# Krishna Cosmic Body

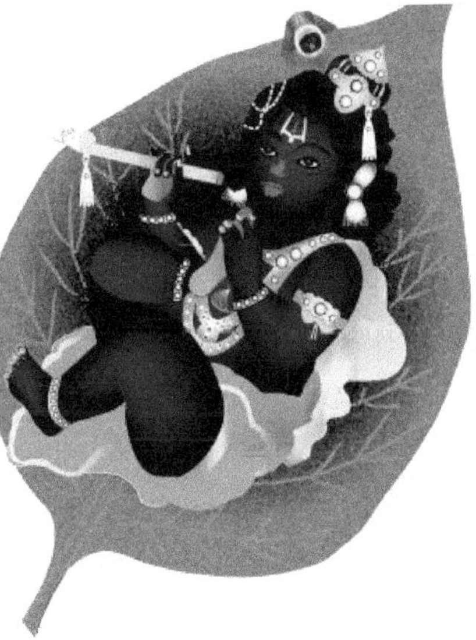

***Michael Beloved***

***(Madhvācārya dās)***

**Published in service to my teachers, Rishi Singh Gherwal and Authur Beverford, who are both deceased*

**Original Sanskrit verse**
Mahabharata: chapters 187-188 Markandeya Samasya Parva of Aranyaka Parva (Vana parva) or 3rd Part.
Electronic text (C) Bhandarkar Oriental Research Institute -- Permission by John Smith

**Devanagari script:** Sanskrit 2003 Font
**Transliteration:** URW Palladio ITU font/ ITranslator
**Word-for-Word typeset:** Michael Beloved
**Proofs Editor:** Marcia Beloved
**Shiva Art:** Sir Paul Castagna
**Illustrations:** Author
**Correspondence:**

Michael Beloved
3703 Foster Ave
Brooklyn NY 11203
USA

Paul Castagna
204 Northern sophie
Bessemer MI 49911
USA

**Email:** axisnexus@gmail.com



**ISBN**
**978-0-9840013-2-3**
**LCCN**
**2012900736**

**Narrative**
Sanskrit Text

**ENGLISH**
Transliteration / Word-for-Word Meaning
**TRANSLATION**

# Table of Contents

# Scheme of Pronunciation

## Consonants

| | | | | | |
|---|---|---|---|---|---|
| Gutturals: | क | ख | ग | घ | ङ |
| | ka | kha | ga | gha | ṅa |
| Palatals: | च | छ | ज | झ | ञ |
| | ca | cha | ja | jha | ña |
| Cerebrals: | ट | ठ | ड | ढ | ण |
| | ṭa | ṭha | ḍa | ḍha | ṇa |
| Dentals: | त | थ | द | ध | न |
| | ta | tha | da | dha | na |
| Labials: | प | फ | ब | भ | म |
| | pa | pha | ba | bha | ma |

**Semivowels:**

| | | | |
|---|---|---|---|
| य | र | ल | व |
| ya | ra | la | va |

**Numbers:**

| | | | | | | | | | |
|---|---|---|---|---|---|---|---|---|---|
| ० | १ | २ | ३ | ४ | ५ | ६ | ७ | ८ | ९ |
| 0 | 1 | 2 | 3 | 4 | 5 | 6 | 7 | 8 | 9 |

| | | | | | |
|---|---|---|---|---|---|
| **Sibilants:** | श | ष | स | **Aspirate:** | ह |
| | śa | ṣa | sa | | ha |

**Vowels:**

| | | | | | | | |
|---|---|---|---|---|---|---|---|
| अ | आ | इ | ई | उ | ऊ | ऋ | ॠ |
| a | ā | i | ī | u | ū | ṛ | ṝ |
| ए | औ | ओ | औ | ळ | ॡ | ं | : |
| e | ai | o | au | lṛ | lṝ | ṁ | ḥ |

**Apostrophe** ऽ

## *How to use this book:*

*Make a casual reading page for page without becoming stressed about the concepts and ideas. Read to become familiar with the language style and presentation. If you read something of particular interest make a mental note of it and read on to get through the entire book.*

*Make a second reading pausing at areas of interest, where you feel you can grasp the material. Here and there, you may not follow the meanings but read on nevertheless.*

*Make a third reading with intent to grasp the concepts and suggestions given.*

*Finally, make an indepth study of this information.*

## ***A note on the diacritical marks and pronounciation:***

*A name like Krishna is accepted in common English usage. Its English spelling has no diacritical marks.*

*Sanskrit letters with a* **dot** *under them, should be pronounced while the tongue touches and is released curling slightly at the top of palate.*

*The* **s** *sound for* **ś** *carries an* **h** *with it and is said as the* **sh** *sound in* **she**.

*The* **s** *sound for* **ṣ** *carries an* **h** *with it and is said as the* **sh** *sound in* **shun**.

*The* **h** *sound for* **ḥ** *carries an echoing sound of the vowel before it, such that* **oḥ** *is actually* **oho** *and* **aḥ** *is actually* **aha**.

*In many Sanskrit words the* **y** *sound is said as an* **i** *sound, especially when the* **y** *sound preceeds an* **ā**. *For instance,* **prāṇāyāma** *should be* **praa-nai-aa-muh**, *rather than* **praa-naa-yaa-muh**.

*The* **a** *sound is more like* **uh** *in English, while the* **ā** *sound is like the* **a** *sound in* **far**.

*The* **ṛ** *sound is like the* **ri** *sound in* **ridge**.

*The* **ph** *sound is never reduced to an* **f** *sound as in English. The* **p** *sound is maintained.*

*Whenever* **h** *occurs after a consonant, its integrity is maintained as an air forced sound.*

*If the* **h** *sound occurs after a vowel and a consonant, one should let the consonant remain with the vowel which preceeds it and allow the* **h** *sound to carry with the vowel after it, such that Duryodhana is pronounced with the* **d** *consonant allied to the* **o** *before it and the* **h** *sound manages the* ***a*** *after it. Say* **Dur-yod-ha-na** *or* **Dur-yod-han**. *Do not say* **Dur-yo-dha-na**. *Separate the* **d** *and* **h** *sounds to make them distinct. In words where you have no choice and must combine the* **d** *and* **h** *sound, as in the word* **dharma**. *Make sure that the* **h** *sound is heard as an air sound pushed out from the throat. Dharma should never be mistaken for darma. But* **adharma** *should be* **ad-har-ma**.

*The* **c** *sound is* **ch**, *and the* **ch** *sound is* **ch-h**.

# Introduction

*Krishna's Cosmic Body is a story of a yogi mystic who witnessed the dissolution of the world, not just the planets but the cosmos as he perceived it. In that situation there was a vast cosmic sea and an atmosphere above it. The waves of the sea were raging and the storm in the atmosphere was terrible and threatening.*

*This yogi floated about here and there, encountering aquatic monsters now and again. After sometime he became tired but there was no land in sight. The upheaval in the deep water did not permit him to rest.*

*He then saw a giant banyan tree standing out of the water. To his surprise there was a male infant lying happily on a giant leaf which seemed to be tied to that tree. He swam near the infant and questioned the child.*

*Soon after, this yogi whose name was Markandeya, found himself being drawn into the mouth of the supernatural infant. Within the body of the divine boy, he found the same world which was inundated outside the body of the boy. Markandeya was struck with wonder since he found familiar persons, places and things within the boy's body.*

*After one hundred years transpired, he was thrown out of the body of the infant. Again he saw the infant as before, lying on the floating banyan leaf. He questioned the boy about the reality of those creations.*

*This story is told in the 3rd. part of the Mahabharata, the Aranyaka Parva, when King Yudhishthira questioned the yogi Markandeya.*

# Chapter 1

## Cosmic Survivor

This narrative is from the Mahabharata tale of activities of the Kuru dynastic civil war. King Yudhishthira, who was ideal social behavior personified, approached the celebrated mystic yogi Markandeya and inquired of ancient history because Markandeya was known to be the oldest living person.

Yudhishthira was the eldest of the Pandava princes who were disinherited from their ancestral kingdom by their cousins who became known as the Kauravas.

The Kauravas were crafty politicians who wanted to rule the ancestral territory with the Pandavas in subordination. Duryodhan, the eldest of the Kaurava princes, was assisted by his maternal uncle Shakuni, who was an expert dice handler.

They challenged Yudhishthira to a game of dice with the intention of having Yudhishthira stake his claim on the kingdom in the dice game. Due to the rules of political forfeiture at the time, Yudhishthira could either play and risk his claim or refuse the challenge and lose it outright.

Stating that it was unfair for a person's uncle to play on his behalf, Yudhishthira agreed to play the game. Time and again Yudhishthira lost with a bad throw of the dice. He lost his stake on the kingdom. Then he wagered his four brothers, then himself and then his wife.

Duryodhan for his part enjoyed this humiliation of Yudhishthira since it was stipulated that upon losing,

Yudhishthira and his brothers would be banished for thirteen years.

During the period of banishment, Yudhishthira met Markandeya, a great yogi who was reputed to be the oldest human being anywhere. Many fantastic tales were told to Yudhishthira by Markandeya but the one which this book recites has to do with the proof Markandeya provided about Krishna being the Supreme Personality, the maintainer and psychological support structure of all the beings in the universe.

Markandeya was reputed to be the eldest person in the world, except for the Procreator Brahmā, who according to this system of cosmology has the appointed task to produce the mundane creation which we perceive. Brahmā is an agent of the actual God of the world, who is identified in this dialog as Krishna.

The value of Markandeya is that he survived a cosmic flood and lived to see the world in its re-created phase. His claim is that he saw the ultimate deity who is the master of the agent deity, Brahmā. Krishna protects Brahmā's existence when Brahmā goes into a cosmic sleep.

In addressing Markandeya, Yudhishthira said this:

***"O great yogi–philosopher no one besides you has witnessed the termination of thousands of time cycles. There is no one in this cosmos who is your equivalent in lifespan or who is as knowledgeable, besides the supreme person, deity Brahmā, who is supremely intelligent."***

The essential point is that a person's lifespan is gauged not by the duration of life but by the memory capacity in the person's psyche. If a man for instance is some 72 years of age and if he cannot remember his previous activities for the last 20 years, then existentially speaking his life span is just 52 years of age. But there are various types of memory, even instinct might serve as memory now and again.

In terms of defense, instinct is a very reliable form of memory. Some wild animals keep a distance from human beings, even from humans who have never attacked them. Their memory as instinct alerts them to the potential danger based on memory factors which now serve as instinct in their psyches.

Markandeya was using vivid recall which is not an instinct but which is a psychic mechanism which can convert previously stored impressions into a video display in the imagination faculty of the mind. This type of memory is more exact and reliable than instinct.

Even though it is believed and even advocated that Markandeya was using a material body which was thousands of years old, this type of memory with which he is attributed is part of a yoga siddha subtle body. It does not operate in a material body, unless the yogi who has that material form also has a yoga siddha form interspaced into it.

It is irrelevant really as to whether Markandeya was using a physical form because the memory of events from thousands of years in the past cannot be supported by a material body unless there is a subtle body interspaced into that material form. It is the subtle body which is capable of supporting such long-ranged recall.

To communicate to persons who are focused through a material body, one has to take a material body or one has to use the services of someone who has such a body. In that sense Markandeya's material form has significance.

But all the same if a student of yoga can develop subtle perception then that student can communication with others who are on the subtle plane and who do not have material bodies.

In this exchange with Yudhishthira, Markandeya used a material body but it is his subtle siddha form which provided the recollection.

Yudhishthira explained more when he said:

***"When the world was without sky, without appointed deities and without the sorcerers who oppose the deities, you alone, O educated mystic, attended the deity Brahmā during the cosmic dissolution."***

This information is based on what was believed at the time in India, among the so called Aryan people in North India. According to their information, there is a Procreator Deity named Brahmā who is a creator-agent for a higher Deity named Nārāyaṇa (Naa-rai-aan-a). This Brahmā created the universe but after some time, he became drowsy. When he finally fell asleep, this cosmic system collapsed. Since the existential energy of the living beings depended on the conscious upkeep of this Brahmā deity, his mental collapse caused their existence to be suspended for some time.

The existences were not destroyed in entirety but went into spiritual latency. When this Brahmā awoke he invoked the creation. Everyone came alive sequentially and entered the history of this place.

Yudhishthira heard from others, that Markandeya, the great mystic yogi, survived the previous dissolution of the world which meant that he survived even when the Procreator Brahmā went to sleep and all the other living beings lost objectivity because of Brahmā's mental collapse.

According to this information, when the Procreator falls asleep everyone else suffers from a loss of self-awareness because all living beings depend on the waking energy of Brahmā for objectivity. Somehow or the other, Markandeya remained awake while this deity slept.

We may try to consider this in terms of the situation of a mother and her embryo. If the embryo is reliant on the mental energy of the mother, then of course if the mother sleeps, the infant will also fall asleep regardless of its desire. Of course we know that while a mother doses, her embryo may carry out activities which indicate that it is not that reliant on the waking consciousness of the mother. But still, studying the feedback between an embryo and its mother, could give some insight into the possibility of what Yudhishthira explained about Markandeya.

Yudhishthira said:

***After the cosmic dissolution reached the stage of universal dormancy, and the great cosmic father became aware, you were the only one who perceived his visualization of the living beings.***

According to this, there were two beings existing when the world was put out of commission, these were the Creator-god Brahmā and the advanced mystic yogi Markandeya. While Brahmā slept, the world which relied on his consciousness was shut down, retrogressed into dormancy.

Because of mystic insight Markandeya saw what transpired in the mind of Brahmā when Brahmā was aroused. He perceived the gradual visualization of the world of living beings which Brahmā's mind constructed as he awoke from the sleeping state. Of course Brahmā might have dreamt but this was not told to Yudhishthira.

This is not that difficult to grasp since we all experience sleeping and waking and the twilight period in between. A person usually repossesses his or her focus when aroused. Gradually or rapidly whatever that person was focused on before going to sleep may again come to mind and the person may resume his or her considerations.

Yudhishthira accredited the Creator-deity Brahmā in this way:

***O self-realized yogi who is an educated ritual priest, the four types of beings were produced by the one who is supremely intelligent. Having put the air and elements in all directions, he scattered water here and there.***

Markandeya was an educated, qualified ritual priest who could invoke supernatural beings for interviews. He was not a primitive superstitious person.

The four types of beings are those which take birth from a womb, from an egg, from moisture and those which sprout from established life forms.

Brahmā is rated as being supremely intelligent because everyone else lives by using a tiny portion of the sum-total intelligence which is in the psyche of Brahmā.

From Brahmā's mental-mystic actions, creative elements inside and outside his psyche were activated into potent energy from which the worlds which depended on Brahmā's mind were created.

Brahmā did not draft a plan, as an architect would. Rather he used potent imagination and spontaneously affected the void condition of his mind. That was sufficient to start the universe.

This is a precise statement about the respect which Markandeya gave Brahmā even though Markandeya developed the power to transcend Brahmā's sleeping respite. There is another story which relates to this, where two male beings, very powerful sorcerers, developed this same transcendental skill to outlive the deity Brahmā. These were Madhu and Kaitabha who.

had a plan to confiscate the memory and creative skill from the mind of Brahmā while he fell asleep.

When a person slumbers, even a deity as powerful as Brahmā, there is at a certain stage a release of the core-self from the adjuncts of the psyche. These adjuncts are the sense of identity, the intellect, the memory chambers, random sensual energy and the life force. Madhu and Kaitabha studied psychology and penetrated their psyches to such a degree that they knew how the system of sleep-release operates.

Understanding that they did not have the creative ability of Brahmā and that he would not award it to them, they devised a plan to seize it from him when he would fall asleep. In contrast however we see that Markandeya was a person with a different character, having no interest in taking advantage of Brahmā's sleeping condition. Markandeya did not desire to have Brahmā's creative skills.

Instead of attempting to outsmart Brahmā, Markandeya linked his consciousness to Brahmā's in a very reverential way. Yudhishthira described this as follows:

***The spiritual master of the world, the great father of the beings, was directly worshipped by you, O best of the initiated ritualists, by your continuous effortless linkage of attention to the highest level of consciousness.***

Since he has that reverence for the creator-god, Markandeya was blessed to remain unaffected by death, old age and even the wholesale destruction of bodies in times of wars and natural disasters when many living beings lose bodies. That was described by Yudhishthira in this way:

***Thus, O self-realized yogi who is an educated ritualist, by the grace of the supremely intelligent person, the***

***termination of everything, death, or old age even, the destruction of all bodies, does not affect you.***

Markandeya is special because he witnessed the dissolution along with the corresponding sleeping condition of the creator-god. The yogi's consciousness was so subtle, precise and keen, that the cosmic subconscious existence was realized objectively by him. Still, he had no desire to exploit the situation. Yudhishthira said this about the yogi:

***When not even the sun, nor fire, nor air, nor the moon, nor even the atmosphere, nor the earth remained; when in this world, there is one ocean, when the stationary and moving creatures were destroyed, as well as the lower deities, the groups of celestial beings and the great serpents become motionless; when the boundless self, the person whose residence is the lotus flower, laid down on the lotus, you alone of all the living beings attended to that deity Brahmā.***

This boundless self is Brahmā. Even though he is just the local creator-god and even though there is someone greater than him, in comparison to the individual living beings who exist in his consciousness, Brahmā is infinite. In comparison to the trillions of limited spirit selves which are in his aura, Brahmā is a god in his own right. Thus Markandeya offered due respect to him.

Yudhishthira, though a prince, was a capable mystic, and still he offered credit to Markandeya, a simple yogi who was so accomplished in objectifying what is subconscious and unconscious, that even the mental condition of the creator-deity Brahmā did not affect him and he remained awake through the sleeping period of that deity.

Yudhishthira made this requested of Markandeya:

*You have superior perception of what occurred before, O best of the initiated ritualists, therefore I wish to hear everything about the essential causes.*

*O best of the initiated ritualists, you alone are knowledgeable about the multiple causes. There is nothing unknown to you about the perpetual situations of these worlds.*

# Chapter 2

## Living in Someone's Dream

Being petitioned by Yudhishthira, Markandeya narrated what he experienced. He presented it as evidence of Krishna's divinity. Markandeya began the response with this:

***This is wonderful. Offering devoted respects to the self-born person, the ancient personality, who is eternal and who is impenetrable, I will explain everything to you.***

The self-born person is Brahmā, the local creator-god who is a deity in his own right. He does however have a superior as we will read further in the discourse.

Markandeya was aware of Brahmā's superior and had communicated with this God directly, and still Markandeya held Brahmā in high regard and never made an effort to undermine the authority of the local deity.

This really means that even if one achieves contact with the Supreme Being, one must still respect others who are lesser authorities. If one fails to do so, then it means that one has lost touch with the system of divine empowerment.

An empowered being is not supreme. That is certain. Still one should offer due respect and not use the information about or relationship with the Supreme Being as a way of neglecting those who serve the supreme and who are in a lesser category.

In so far as a lesser being serves the mission of the Supreme Person, that lesser person is due for respect and honor. If one slights such a being when that person functions as a servant of the Supreme, one will have to absorb a negative consequence for the neglect.

One has a great advantage if one can learn how to recognize God's power in others, even when the others are in an inferior category.

After appraising the creator-deity, Markandeya appraised Krishna as the Grand Deity, the maintainer of the living beings. Krishna was present physically. Brahmā was absent and yet, Markandeya offered respect to Brahmā fully and then turned his attention to Krishna, whom he identified as the Primal Person:

***This person with wide long eyes and yellow garments is Krishna Janārdana, the maintainer of the beings, the agent and transformer, the one who is the activator of all creatures and existences.***

These salutations are also leveled at Brahmā, the subordinate creator-deity, but when used for Krishna in this case, it over-rides the significance of Brahmā. This will be explained elsewhere. Krishna is described further:

***He is inconceivable, full of wonder, pure, the best, without beginning or ending, the substance, the world, undeteriorating and unchanging.***

***This person is the producer but he is not produced by anyone. He is the cause of personal power. Indeed, this person knows but the lower deities do not know him.***

This is Markandeya's opinion based on his experiences with Krishna previously when Brahmā's consciousness was asleep. Markandeya gave his direct view and not hearsay about Krishna. This is a personal estimation about the importance of Krishna, the physical person who was with Yudhishthira at the time of this discourse.

Markandeya is direct. Since his evidence is his experience, we do not get the usual, "He said this." Or, "He mentioned this." Markandeya narrated what he witnessed during the dissolution:

***O best of kings, tiger among men, after the destruction of the world, all of this wonderful creation, which was without manifestation, begins again.***

Right now, at this time in history, our scientists are aggressively prying into the affairs of the universe, to figure when it began, how long will be its development and what it will become in dissolution. Obviously, Markandeya had the same curiosity but he used mystic means to investigate.

The first thing is evident which is that the world is manifested. We are sure about that because of sensual perception. Science has also speculated that a collapse of this universe would be the very same reason for a rebirth of it either in this same existential space or in some other cosmic gap.

Where does the energy go when the universe collapses? Does it become unmanifest? Does it become dark matter? Does it become invisible?

When and if it is initiated again either by a deity or just by the nature of energy, then do the same beings manifest in it again? Or is that next set of beings new characters?

The duration of creation is split into various eras with each succeeding time-span being reduced by a factor of one quarter. If the first time cycle is said to have four thousand years, then the next will have three thousand years, followed by another with two thousand years and a last concluding one with one thousand years. But these years are not the solar years we endure.

Markandeya described that in this way:

***It is said that four thousand years is the duration of the Era of Easy Achievement. This includes hundreds of dawns and evenings which come one after another.***

***Three thousand years is said to be the duration of the Treta Era. Of this there are hundreds of initial stages and terminations in sequence.***

***Similarly, there is the Dvāpara Era which is for two thousand years in duration. This has initial stages and terminations occurring in sequence for two hundred years.***

***For a duration of one thousand years, the next is the Kali Era. So it is known. This has sequential initial stages and terminations each lasting one hundred years. Understand that the duration of an initial stage and termination are the same.***

Neither of these years are human years which are based on the earth's rotation around the sun. Within each of these grand eras, there are sub-timespans in which conditions and methods of culture vary being reinforced, being upgraded or being degraded.

The least of the eras is the Kali era which is the most degrading. Each Kali era except for the very last one in a time cycle, is followed by a full upgrade to the most elevating time which is the Age of Easy Achievement, the *Kṛta Yuga.* After the very last Kali era, there is a cosmic catastrophe such that the whole system collapses. All living beings except for Brahmā and his Deity, cease to exist for the time being. Then the *Kṛta Yuga,* which is also called the *Satya Yuga,* commences again.

This is the time in which people perceive this existence in the real way knowing that it is a temporary manifestation from which one could transit to an eternal spiritual environment. It is known as the Age of Easy Achievement because accurate psychic, supernatural and spiritual perception is a natural part of the perception faculties of many of the human forms in that Age.

The year count in these durations is the year of the supernatural people in the celestial world. Their time reference is different. In fact one year for us equals to just one day for them. One year for them is 360 years for us. This is not just fantasy and myth. If one experienced astral projection, one will know that time varies according to the dimension.

Markandeya explained:

***In the termination of the Kali Era, the Age of Easy Achievement commences again. A cycle of these Eras is twelve thousand years.***

According to this the least of the eras, the Kali Age, lasts for 1200 years of the celestial people which is 1200 x 360 or 432,000 human years. In each of these eras, there is a particular dominant influence which causes a spiritual upgrade or psychological deterioration.

The situation of Brahmā is different to that of other supernatural rulers. Hence Markandeya gave a clarification:

***One thousand complete cycles is said to be a day in the life of the deity Brahmā. Indeed when this universe retrogresses into the existence of deity Brahmā, the accomplished yogis say that the world is in cosmic dissolution, O tiger of men.***

The situation of Brahmā is fabulous when compared to humanity. It is more like: We live as micro-beings in a daydream of Brahmā. If I am in someone's daydream and if my being is made of the substance of that person's imagination, then how am I to gage the dreamer's sense of time?

Some people are very particular to say that they are worshipping the Supreme God, not some paltry under-pin of the deity, not some sub-agent. But does it really matter if I am in love with a sub-deity or with the Supreme Being? What is the difference except that I can boast of my attraction to the Supreme when it really may not apply to me if I am existentially reliant on the sub-agent?

Brahmā lives for one hundred years but his time rate is different. During those one hundred years, he has days and nights just as we do, except that the durations for him are fabulous in comparison.

At the end of each of his days, he takes rest, but that implies a cancellation of our existences. It may be said that certain cells in the brain experience a cancellation of functions when my body sleeps. But those same cells again participate in the body's history when I awake.

When Brahmā sleeps our existences are suspended. When he awakens we discover ourselves as functions in consciousness again. It is even presented elsewhere in the Vedic literature, that periodically Brahmā falls asleep in the middle of one of his days. He takes a nap. Whenever he does, our situations are instantly suspended. When he becomes self-conscious again, we also find that our existence is real.

Even though Brahmā is not the Supreme Being, still, our objective consciousness is reliant on his. If a part of a dream ceases to exist the dreamer may still continue dreaming. But if the dreamer ceases to dream, those who were created as part of his mental display will be de-existed instantly.

Some people are of the opinion that if they worship the Supreme Being, they will avoid being blanked out by a sub-deity. But this idea is ludicrous. It is a puny but rather failed attempt to transcend one's existential fate.

The relevance of this was settled long ago in the paradox which Chuang Tzu found himself while living in a body as a Chinese some two thousand years ago. He dreamt that he was a butterfly but then he was not certain if it was his dream or if he was the subject of the dream of the butterfly.

If I am a subject in the dream of a deity, then for me that deity is God. There is no point in thinking that I would be greater if I were to make contact with the person in whose mind, my deity was merely part of a dream.

# Chapter 3

## Degrading Social Conditions

In each of the eras, a particular set of influences prevails. Human beings may resist these trends. Those who are inclined to a righteous lifestyle resist vices which are habits which cause them to be degraded to either a lower behavior or to a lower species of life.

The last of the eras, the Kali era, is the time when a devilish supernatural being prevails. His influence supports financial leverage for exploiting others, intoxication for developing insensitivity for social responsibility, encouragement for gambling away one's hard earned income, insensitive conscience about social morality and easy facility to continue primitive eating habits in a modern human body.

Markandeya gave a briefing about the trends which usually prevail in the Kali era:

***Then at the end of an era, when a small part of it remains, O best of the Bharatas, at the end of the thousand years, the people in general become untruthful in speech.***

This is a preview of what happens in the final Kali era, just before deity Brahmā falls asleep at the end of his day. There are many Kali eras or times of devilish influence, but this final one has a total breakdown in the social as well as environmental situations.

In the case of a social breakdown with environmental stability, there is some hope for reform but when there is both social and environmental collapse, social renovation does not occur.

The process takes a certain course. It spirals downwards rapidly. This is what Markandeya explained:

***At the time, O son of Pṛthā, religious ceremonies are performed by proxy agents, and gifts are given in the same way as well as commitments which are made by substitute agents.***

***Religious leaders and philosophers do the social work of laborers. Laborers act like those who usually focus on acquiring wealth. In the course of the era, those who should have the righteous lifestyle of the government administrators abandon that.***

***Ceasing speciality in knowledge and Vedic study, not offering food and water ceremonially to ancestors, the priestly and philosophically-inclined persons become carnivorous in the Kali Era.***

This is related to the caste structure in India, where society was to be tiered according to four employment aptitudes. These four were teachers, political administrators, commercially-minded people and laborers. In time, this caste system was criticized. For instance in our time, it is all but abolished even though in some parts of India it is still maintained as an undercurrent in a free society.

The teachers were in the highest caste which was that of the brahmins who either taught religious procedures or secular matters of speciality. The political administrators were in the next caste. These were the ksatriyas. In ancient India, these ksatriyas were a warrior caste. They governed society through the formation of ruling families and tribal chieftains. Then there was the mercantile caste which was families specializing in trade. The last of the socially-tiered segments was the laborers, the shudras. There was also an undeclared outcaste sector which was anyone who did not fit into this social schematic, especially aborigine peoples and foreigners.

Because of the rigidity of the four castes, and because of the human tendency for exploitation and suppression, the caste system was highly criticized. Eventually it was banned in India.

It continues in India however. It also continues elsewhere but under the guise of class structure instead of caste structure. With the removal of family discrimination, there arose economic and ethnic discrimination and the prejudices function through that means.

What happened is that initially when these castes were set up among the Aryan people it was a fair system for mutual well-being based on employment aptitude. People reincarnated in family lines which were conducive of and facilitating of their particular social aptitudes but eventually this orderly routing through reincarnation changed for the worse.

Subsequently the teachers and the administrators hired the other castes to do their work. This meant that wealth and status which gave the two higher castes leverage caused them to become lazy in executing duties.

Instead of doing a religious ceremony himself for instance, a brahmin taught someone from one of the other castes and paid that person to perform a religious ceremony. This worked in that it produced a feeling of expansion and growth for that brahmin. Now instead of doing about three ceremonies per day, he could do six or more ceremonies per day if he hired enough unqualified persons at a cheap rate to do ceremonies on his behalf.

The benefit was money, something that the brahmin caste always lacked before this expansion. Now instead of having to wait on administrators to build large temples, the brahmins themselves collected vast sums of money and built shrines. They became World Teachers or Jagat Gurus instead of being simple forest ascetics on the outskirts of civilization or instead of being supported as a dynastic priest for a wealthy ruling family.

As soon as the brahmin caste becomes perverted with expansion of power and prominence, all other castes are affected in a negative way. Thus society takes a down turn. This however is not realized because for every aspect which deteriorates, something else is gained as an advantage.

The brahmin caste gained independence in terms of income. Instead of depending on donations, they directly collected funds. The administrative caste was relieved of having to negotiate currency through businessmen. They no longer treated laborers as dependents. They sold goods and directly generated funds. They did work which previously was monopolized by laborers.

The businessmen advanced themselves as politicians or teachers. They were no longer restricted to trade and agricultural management. The laborers got the privilege of entering the three higher castes which were off-limits previously. The advantages are clear to see but these elevations were flawed. Many human beings are unable to effectively maneuver across the social chasms.

Markandeya then explained how people began to move out of their caste station into higher categories while a corresponding group of persons from higher caste, moved into lower status:

***My dear, the brahmins do not recite sacred sounds, while the laborers become devoted to recitation. Then in the world, everything goes to the contrary, and there is destruction as before.***

As the time cycles wind down, people who were stuck in the lower castes, who took birth after birth in peasant families, begin looking for ways of moving upwards to enjoy the spoils of the earth, and to get the opportunity to govern themselves and others.

Some carried lives of resentment for being mistreated by the higher castes. This energy vented itself during political unrest and full-scale social revolution. Some of the teacher caste and some of the administrative caste, become rebellious leaders of persons from the lower castes who desire opportunities to teach, govern and manage finances.

Both fair and unfair persons from the two higher castes become afraid of being killed, tortured or imprisoned by persons from the lower castes who threaten to upset the status quo.

In India where brahmins specialized in technical Vedic sounds of the Sanskrit language, they abandoned the pronunciation speciality of their family clans and gave over the worship ceremonies to anyone from the lower castes who showed an interest.

This relieved the brahmins from the resentments of the lower classes and gave the brahmins the opportunity to live in a carefree way without respect to the various stipulations for hygiene, cultivation of scriptural knowledge, introspective study of psychic reality, performance of worship ceremonies and having to set the example in morality to a critical public.

Markandeya elaborated:

***O ruler of human beings, many kings of the uncultured classes will rule over the earth. These persons being devoted to propaganda will condition the people to dishonesty and criminal activities.***

***The Āndhra, Śaka, Pulinda, Yavana, Kāmbojā, Aurṇika, and Abhīra tribesmen who are the equivalent of laborers, will prevail O best of the human beings.***

The idea is that over time, after many eras pass, after many souls transmigrate though various species, and especially in the human form of life, much resentment will accumulate as a soul moves from one species to another. Even within the confines of one species, the various entities will resent one another and will fight viciously for dominance.

One group who is in a lower caste or class will act defiantly, assess their social power and challenge the rulers. Someone from a lower caste or class will take over the country's finances and rule with an iron hand.

Someone on the pretext of working for civil rights or for freedom from oppression, will take power and then declare himself as president for life, thus effectively doing the very same thing which he promised to free his fellows from.

Restrictions which were placed on certain segments of the population, especially on the lower classes and which were enforced unfairly will be lifted by those who seize power. In that way they will relieve their fellows even though they will not have the purity and authority to insist on fair policy and ideal behavior.

Even though Yogi Markandeya named certain tribesmen who were present in India at the time of the discourse with Yudhishthira, the yogi himself is not prejudiced but he was aware of the upward thrust of evolution which forces those on the lower end of the human cultural spectrum to branch out courageously and claim a higher role.

In the Age of Easy Achievement *(Kṛta / Satya Yuga)*, people more or less remained in their caste because the environment did not sponsor anything but gradual evolutionary upliftment over many many lives. Even the animals were included in this gradual escalator scheme of material nature. Still, as the ages rolled by, people from the lower castes and classes, developed familiarity with the higher castes and classes and desired to assume higher social roles in society.

As nature would prefer it, those who were aborigines remained in that sort of life in many many births, repeatedly dying, taking birth, dying and taking birth again in the same tribe. But when such persons were hired or forced to serve the higher castes or classes, they got insight about the functions and skills of their rulers and wished to be elevated.

These wishes developed into full-blown desire which nature responded to and thus presented opportunities for elevation either by methods which further stabilized society or by violent upheavals which ravaged countries.

At the end of the Age of Easy Achievement some advanced beings stop taking human bodies. They transit to higher planes of existence and are removed from the evolutionary pressures which come from material nature and which scroll out time and history in physical existence.

Some advanced entities do stay on and ride it out through the gradual but certain deterioration of the environment and social situations.

The Kali Era is a hell-hole for one and all but it is in a sense a great opportunity for those who are down-trodden, for the unskilled and uneducated sectors of humanity. The very last Kali Era in a time cycle, which comes at the end of Brahmā's day, just at the time when he is drowsy and will soon fall asleep, is a very negative environment:

***Then not one priestly and philosophically-minded person remains committed to the righteous lifestyle for that caste. O king of human beings, the administrators and their assistants and the mercantile people engage in deviant activities.***

***People will have short lifespan, very little strength, little vitality and much less heroism. They will have stunted bodies, little power, and be reduced in truthful speech.***

No matter how great one is, one is still dependent on a favorable environment. If nature itself becomes hostile, then it does not matter who one is or what one desires, one will see hell.

We must understand that there are two factors which interplay. These are the social environment of Nature and the psychic environment of the individual living entity. The social environment is a general influence which prevails upon everyone in human society. The psychic environment is the individual mental and emotional make-up of a particular person. The result of this interaction may be elevating or degrading to the individual. If someone is very resistant to degrading energy, then it is likely that he or she will survive the assault of negative persons and a negative environment.

Markandeya explained:

***The countries become devoid of human beings. Predatory species and wild animals spread in all directions. At the end***

*of the era, even persons who have no carnal knowledge are degraded. The laborers call out, 'Hey you!' The priestly and philosophically-minded persons address others saying, 'Yes, Sir.'*

*At the end of the era, there is an increase in animals. O tiger of men. Also, all odors and essential oils are not as consumable. O king, flavors are not as sweet when sensually detected.*

*There are many children with dwarf bodies, and lacking good character and behavior. O king, the women's mouths function as vaginas when it is the destruction of the era.*

*The residences of the citizens will be without food; highways will be littered with prostitutes; women will be immodest, O king, at the end of the time cycle.*

*Cows produce little milk, O king. The trees filled with many crows, produce very little flowers and fruits.*

Essentially this means that Nature itself will become hostile to human dignity. Environmental conditions will be disagreeable. It will be very hard to survive. Physical existence on planet earth and even in the astral dimensions which are adjacent to the earth will be like hell.

The statement about women's mouths functioning as vaginas is significant because the female sexual facility is valuable as the entrance to and the exit from the initial creation of a body, of an embryo.

In the human species, Nature assigned the body of the woman for the development of the human embryo. That one facility makes the female reproductive organs a most valuable asset for humanity. If we lose sight of this, we inflict on ourselves serious injury.

One should always consider if one may ever again require a human body. If that ever happens again, one will have to rely on the reproductive organs of a female human being. In the light of that, one should respect that function accordingly. It does not matter if one is male or female, the reliance on the female reproductive organ remains.

Markandeya gave special emphasis to the teacher caste, the so called brahmins. Incidentally the Sanskrit word for brahmin, which is *brahmāṇa*, is derived from the Sanskrit words *brahmā* and *brahmān*. Both words mean the Supreme Being, the Supreme Reality, the ultimate level of existence. To be a brahmin, one should be familiar with the Absolute Truth, the Cause of all causes, irrespective of whether that reality is personal or impersonal or comprising both features as its reality.

Emphasis must be given to the teacher caste or class because of their position of influence in human society. Their malfunction was described by Markandeya:

***O ruler of the earth, the certified ritual priests, being faulted by their killing of the priestly and philosophical persons, will take favors from politicians who are expert at propaganda.***

***Being possessed by greed and impractical ideas, exhibiting pretentious religious principles and saintly insignia, the ritual experts travel here and there in various directions. O protector of the earth, they pose as being worthy of religious donations.***

In the time of Markandeya, the teachers were primarily teachers of religious doctrine along Vedic lines. As in the history of the West, religious learning by aural means was principal before the predominance of the printing press. Education was mostly theological learning with historic overtones.

As this developed, history of dynasties took precedence even over religion. In primitive societies, elders ruled by religious influence mostly but when these elders organize their family clans into dynasties, the history of those families becomes part of the education process.

Thus we find that the two most powerful means of influence even in human society today are religion and ideology. Ideology is the modern word for political indoctrination. Gradually over time political history eclipsed and then totally overshadowed religious history. Political history is realistic while religious history is inclusive of superstition and abstract ideas which cannot be verified physically.

When human society begins to develop in nation states, religious leaders are challenged with the choice of allying themselves to political leaders or losing influence over the masses of people. Those who make friendship with the politicians become prominent. The others are reduced and maintain small groups of followers with little or no influence over human history.

Those who make friends with politicians must do their best to eliminate the more sincere religious leaders either by killing them or by muting them with propaganda. Humanity is forever looking for an easy way out of its dilemmas and thus religious leaders, who advertise an easy method of salvation, are usually successful in getting a large following.

Politicians find this to be convenient since by converting one religious leader they are assured of the support of his numerous followers. In this way religion and politics operate in unison to control and manage humanity.

In some political processes like communism, religion and politics are fused. The state fills in for God. The leader of the party fills in as the minister and president, and the people are herded as one mass body.

In terms of taxation, both religion and politics require money and must tax the citizens in order to effectively operate. Thus politicians and religious leaders sit down and make agreements about the percentage of income taken for the state and the amount required the religious cause. In the communist state, this is simplified as the government absorbs the function of the state and the religion. The masses in the communist state are given a token income after the representatives of the State remove the stipulated taxes.

In the Kali Eras, one of which we are in right now, there is efficient tax collection by governments. In response citizens find ways of avoiding income tax:

***Being fearful of taxes, the people, the married couples, become deceitful. The yogi philosopher assumes a disguise and is forced to depend on commerce for a livelihood.***

In the days when barter was the most efficient way to do trade, governments had elaborate means of checking on the income of the citizens. Kings appointed tax collectors for provinces and counties and used roads and checkpoints as the primary way to tally income and extract tax.

Later humanity developed financially in a way that was more effective for tax collection, which was the use of money instead of barter. A farmer of melons for instance could in ancient times, give over a number of his fruits as a tax to the ruler but nowadays that is not allowed.

Now the farmer must convert the melons to currency and give the government a percentage of that. The burden of the conversion is with the farmer. If he refuses to do so, he may be imprisoned. The state may auction his melons, take the tax stipulated and fine him for non-compliance.

Human nature is inclined to making a profit and so people will do whatever is necessary to decrease the tax and increase their share of the income.

In the time of Markandeya, the yogi philosophers did not have to generate an income. People appreciated these persons to such an extent that sufficient donations were given. These yogis were not greedy, did not have many desires and did not have the urge to exploit others.

Maintaining such a person was a minor expense for anybody of means. Yogis were not considered to be a financial nuisance in society. However nowadays people are mistrustful of religious leaders and even of lone yogis who do not have a congregation. This is because there are many ascetics who are dishonest:

***Then, O tiger among men, the men being pretentious assume nails and hairs of monks. Being greedy for wealth, without purpose, they appear as celibate yogis.***

***In the home of the spiritual teacher, they exhibit degrading behaviors. They become alcoholics and are desirous of having sexual intercourse with those who are related to the spiritual teacher. They are desirous of vulgarity and become prosperous by handling flesh and blood.***

***There will be many scatter-brained people who do not believe in God. They will speak highly of what is contrary and disorderly. O tiger-like man, when the time cycle deteriorates, this will be the situation at the home of the spiritual teacher.***

Religion was always a risky investment for humanity. This is because religion deals with the hereafter, a territory that is invisible to physical sense perception. Thus there is always the chance that a religious leader will be advocating a result which will never be realized.

Since religion deals with the hereafter, it can always exploit the follower since it does not have to deliver the promised result during the physical life. This loophole is exploited by many religious leaders. The fear of death is ever looming in the mind of a human being and thus, humans will always be susceptible to religious exploitation. It is a risk that we must take.

Some moral restrictions need enforcement in human society, even in societies which are primarily atheistic. Morality is concerned with sexual exchange and labor purchase, such that exploitation and advantage are curtailed. Procreative and recreational sex should be restricted so that one party does not rape the other or beget children irresponsibly. The exchange of labor should be monitored so that slavery does not become a reality.

However as humanity winds down in the Kali Age, regulations for controlling sex drive and the rules for discouraging labor exploitation are upset by criminal persons who take control of the religious organizations and governments.

***Then the deity Indra, who subdued Pāka, does not give rain as it should be. Most of the seeds planted in the earth do not develop, O descendant of Bharata. A person becomes involved in a socially-destructive lifestyle which yields the corresponding results exorbitantly, O gentle entity.***

***O protector of the earth, those who are situated in virtuous conduct, have a short lifespan. Indeed the righteous lifestyle is not regarded by anyone.***

The tale of the battle between Indra and Pāka is related in more than one Purana. In the Srimad Bhagavatam it is told in Canto 8. These stories appear to be myths to modern people and thus I decline to go into its details.

However, Indra was considered to be the patron deity of rainfall in the time of Markandeya. Those supernatural beings who opposed Indra or who wanted to usurp his power, were considered to be asuras or resistors. One of these was Pāka, a mighty warrior who was killed by Indra.

One way to consider this is to note that in ancient times, agriculture was completely dependent on seasonal rainfall. Nowadays a farmer might ignore the weather by digging wells and installing sprinklers. Previously most farmers were completely dependent on rainfall. Subsequently there were elaborate rituals conducted to appease supernatural agency for favorable weather.

Even in the time of Krishna, his foster father, Nanda Gopa, was very superstitious about worshipping Indra, who is regarded as the deity who regulates rainfall.

It is irrelevant really if rain is controlled by a supernatural being or if it is controlled merely by atmospheric pressure. In either case, if there is no rainfall, humanity will have difficulty finding food. Even in the modern society, there is some anxiety about rainfall since even if one digs wells, one cannot have water if the water table is low. In fact in some developed countries this is the situation, where there are large pumps for extracting water, but the water level drops lower and lower.

Science is our helper but unless there is rainfall in certain areas, even science becomes crippled in its effort to ease the strain. Markandeya mentioned the non-sprouting of seeds. That is also being addressed currently because of the global use of fertilizers, herbicides and pesticides which after years of usage affect the genetic structure of plants. But we are also uncertain about genetically modified plants and seeds which our agricultural scientists are producing.

The environment itself may become hostile to humanity, and counterproductive to a righteous life style. Nature itself might begin rewarding what is unfair and penalizing what is fair. These conditions will be perplexing for humanity.

In reference to businessmen, Markandeya described their degradation like this:

***The people being desirous of commodities are sold with false economic means. Moreover, businessmen, O tiger-like ruler, operate by dishonest methods.***

***Those who are established in a virtuous lifestyle become distressed. The person who is dishonest thrives. Then there is the loss of power for virtue. As it is, the fraudulent means express authority.***

***At the end of the era, people who are sincere in the practice of righteous lifestyle become short-lived and poverty-stricken; while those who are against righteous conduct have ample income and become well-situated.***

***Moreover, the citizens endeavor by ruse and criminal means. By the accumulation of a little money those who are wealthy become mad with pride.***

Getting rich means that one is able to derive a considerable profit by moving one item from one area, and selling it elsewhere where it is in demand. Before the modern era, this type of activity was very haphazard. With the introduction of electricity and electronics, many businessmen have honed their commercial skills and found ways to increase the margin of profit.

In all respects making a profit has to do with exploiting human labor. It has to do with making an item cheaply in one area and then moving the item for sale to another area where there is demand.

The lever in capitalism is cheap labor but the successful capitalist keeps that aspect hidden because it shows the ugly side of upper classes. A capitalist keeps the public focused on resources and de-focused on labor exploitation. Every so often however, this backfires and people declare that the capitalist does not own the earth's resources.

This however is ineffective. In the democratic states, the capitalist controls the politicians. In the communist system the state assumes the position as the capitalist, which really means that the leader of the party owns all business.

In a capitalist venture, the ugliest part of the enterprise must be hidden. That ugliest part is the asset which is the most exploited. It may be a commodity, a natural resource, employees or the way the items is conveyed to the market.

Whatever it is, it is important that the capitalist keep that hidden from the public. There should be no effective competitors. No one should understand exactly how the profit is made. In fact it is important that the general public be oblivious of the actual sum of money which the capitalist really makes.

Workers must be kept pacified because if they strike, then the flow of commodities comes to a standstill and that is bad for business. The earth's resources must be acquired cheaply, so that the manufactured items can be sold at a reasonable price which is within the public's means.

The idea behind capitalism is to prove that one man, a group of men or a family, is superior to everyone else. Money itself means very little but the power which is derived from it, is the real thing.

In the Kali Era, it happens that Nature seems to favor those who are dishonest. It penalizes those who are fair in dealings. Virtue itself loses power and fraudulent means express great authority. Subsequently people who are righteous become cowards and stand back while the world is controlled by conniving persons and criminals.

Despite the disadvantages in the Kali Era, the Age of Demeaning Behavior, there is a stir which slackens the rigidity of caste and class. This means that someone who in previous eras remained confined to the activities of a specific vocation or the lack of it, may develop some other skill as desired. Over all it is a demeaning Age but it does provide social elevation for some fortunate human beings. Many who move up during this Age are actually moving downwards but they do not understand how this is taking place. Some persons actually move up permanently during this Age when they take opportunities and do not misuse the circumstances.

The tendency to exploit and misuse others is deeply rooted in human nature. Markandeya explained how it would be expressed in the Kali Era:

***Men are eager to confiscate the money entrusted with confidence which was deposited by mutual agreement. Being completely obsessed they figure deceitful methods, declaring that the funds are finished.***

The influence of the Kali Age will also be reflected in the animal kingdom. It is a psychic influence which will penetrate all species of life:

***Cannibals, predators, birds and wild animals lie down in cities, residential places and public assemblies.***

Early sexual maturity and curtailment of the human lifespan will be features near the end of the Kali Era:

***Females of the age of seven and eight will carry fetuses, O King. Males who are ten and twelve will be the father of children.***

***Men become grey-haired in their sixteenth year. Indeed the vitality of people's life deteriorates quickly. This must be endured.***

The relationship of respect for elders will disappear completely. In fact it will manifest in reverse. Irresponsible sexual indulgence will be a factor which carries no moral shame.

***In the end of the era, O great King, youths will assume the temperament of the elderly, while that which is becoming of the youths will be displayed in the people of old age.***

***Then the women secretly do what is contrary by deceiving their husbands. They deviate sexually with criminal characters, servants and even with animals.***

# Chapter 4

## Creator-god Falls Asleep

There are two aspects to existence which are the psychological and the environmental ones. Both have importance even though for introspection purpose, the psychological one is given priority. People who are extrovert are concerned with environmental situations. They neglect the psychological conditions because they can offset those inconveniences by focusing externally, a technique which they master easily.

People who are introvert sometimes overlook the environmental conditions and in some cases, they do so at their peril. This is because in the final analysis one has to exist in an environment, even if the environment is accessed from within the psyche.

To transit to other dimensions, a yogi might access those places from within the psyche but still such places are actually environments. It is not that the yogi goes within and finds within only what is within the psyche. Rather a yogi goes within and finds doorways to other dimensions, other outside environments.

If the yogi's psyche was an elevator, then each floor in the building would be another external environment. The door of the elevators could then give access to each of those other external environments. The yogi could either look out through the glass door or open the door and physically enter into those other environments.

Existence is exactly like this. The problem facing all living beings is twofold:

having the best psychology
living in the best external environment

When social conditions deteriorate, a living being is faced with adversity. This can be tolerated and even transcended. If however there is psychic collapse, then the situation cannot be dismissed as easily.

Markandeya continued the description of the down-turn of social and environment conditions:

***In the end of the thousand-year era, when the lifetime is shortened, there will be a drought, O great king, for several years.***

***Then having little vitality, the living beings become small, reaching their end. Many of them go into the ground, O caretaker of the earth.***

At this point in the development of the Kali Age, Nature itself will turn on the living beings. It will be such that the great outdoors will be hated by living beings. Every creature, human or other, will seek to go underground to get out of the hostile environment.

Markandeya continued:

***Then O ruler of men, seven blazing suns evaporate all water of oceans and rivers.***

***O son of the Bharata family, wood and also grass, dried or wet, all of the natural world in fact, will, O best of the Bharatas, be converted into ashes.***

***Then O descendant of Bharata, solar flares, fires, along with wind, will spread over everything on the earth which was already parched by the sun.***

In terms of life on earth, this will be the end of time. But we must remember that Markandeya described a repeating situation, whereby the solar system comes into existence and goes out of existence and then comes into existence again on the basis of material nature's potential and the Brahmā deity's recurring mental ideas.

This disaster does not touch the core-selves of the living entities but it does destroy their means of manifestation in the material world. The access to this place is temporarily terminated.

The collapse of the system does not occur because of deterioration in human social behavior, even though that does occur. It deteriorates because of Nature's alterations on the physical and psychological planes.

Nature is also psychological. When the creator-god, Brahmā, becomes drowsy, a psychological darkness ensues. This energy is the source of the collapse. Markandeya was immune to this retardative mental force. Others who did not have that capability faced ruination and temporary extinction.

***Then having split the earth, it penetrates to the nether region, producing great terror for the supernatural controllers, the rebellious descendants of Danu and the Yaksha nature spirits.***

***Consuming the realms of the psychic serpents, and any living creature on the ground, it annihilates in a split second all life, O protector of the earth.***

***Then the solar flare, that fire, even the unwelcomed wind, consume hundreds of thousands of 160-mile stretches in distance.***

***That reality, the flame, the spectacular effulgence burns the entire world consisting of devilish entities, celestial musicians, Yaksha nature spirits, uraga snakes and devilish beings.***

At that point, the limited entities who maintained supernatural existences in various supernatural species of life on the astral planes were also annihilated. It was the end of their life-game in that cosmic time phase.

Having fried all the living beings in the material and psychological environments, the energy became converted into massive clouds of cosmic moisture. Without regard to what it had done, the energy vented itself as it become heavier and heavier. It coalesced and rained.

In the meantime, in the mind of the creator-deity, Brahmā, his consciousness shifted from drowsiness to the initial stages of sleep.

***Then massive clouds which are similar to herds of elephants and which are wonderful to see, like decorative garlands, float by in the sky.***

***Some (of those clouds) were colored like the blue lily; some were bluish-blackish; some have the hue of the night-blooming lotus; some like touchstone; some like grass; some are yellow. Some are like milk-laden breasts.***

***Some have the color of turmeric. Some are similar to a crow's eggs. Some look like brightly-colored lotus petals. Some have effulgence being colored like vermillion.***

***Some are like the best constructed cities. Some look like herds of elephants. Some are similar to lizards. Some remain poised like crocodiles. Indeed the clouds expanded and were surcharged with a garland of lightning.***

***O king, initially those terrible cloud formations made rumbling sounds. Then streams of water completely pervaded the sky in all directions.***

***By those clouds, this entire earth with mountains, forest and mines is flooded with water in all directions, O great King.***

This is a cosmic storm which involves the sun splitting and forming new suns which are in a nuclear instability. This is more than physical. This occurs on the psychic plane as well. It is very frightening. If one was to witness this, no amount of bravery could protect one from the fear of this.

The relationship between what took place in the creator-god's mind and what happened in the world is indicated:

***Those terrible clouds roared monstrously, O best of the human beings. As willed by the supreme being, Brahmā, those clouds quickly flooded everywhere.***

***Pouring a vast quantity of rain with streaming downpours, they extinguish those very terrible, inauspicious and horrible wild fires.***

***Then for twelve years water repeatedly rained and flooded; so it was as invoked by the supreme soul.***

***The ocean surpassed its limits, O descendant of the Bharatas. The mountains broke apart. The planet earth was overwhelmed.***

***Then suddenly in all directions, the water was evaporated into the sky. The temptuous winds having surrounded the planet, utterly absorbed everything.***

***Then O ruler of human society, descendant of Bharata, having swallowed the terrible storm winds, the self-produced deity, the one whose bed is the lotus, the god, fell asleep.***

Even though in reference to us, this creator-god Brahmā is inconceivable, still his power is limited. In fact his duration for conscious existence is offset by the need for unconscious states. He cannot keep himself awake forever, just as a human being also cannot stay awake after several sleepless days.

Even on Brahmā's level sleep is mandatory. It is overpowering. Rest is required. This deity willed that it was to rain everywhere even in outer space. However this does not mean that he willed in full consciousness.

He was under the grip of slumber. His will power was confiscated. It willed what it had to will according to the rest-needs of the life force.

When someone is asleep he might signal approval even for things which he does not desire, all because he is not conscious enough to make the proper decisions. At that time, his will power is confiscated by the sleep-energy.

We know that this deity is Brahmā, because he is the one whose bed is a lotus flower. He is said to be self-produced because none of the created entities can transcend his appearance and find his source. They do not have the required insight. They are unable to perceive what happened before they were produced.

Markandeya, a rare super-yogi, was the first limited being who survived Brahmā's drowsy condition and sleep. This happened because Markandeya's awareness was sponsored by the Deity of Brahmā.

Since his mind was now supported by the Primal Deity who transcended Brahmā, Markandeya could observe Brahmā's sleeping condition and the resulting chaos which ensued for all others in the creation.

***In this situation there is one ghastly ocean. The mobile and immobile creatures cease to exist. The beneficent and vindictive supernatural beings are no more. The nature spirits and devilish beings are lacking.***

***O ruler of the earth, without human beings, without wild animals or trees anywhere in the sky or on the earth, I, being the one person there, wandered about in a troubled state of mind.***

***O best of the kings of the earth, while wandering in that terrible ocean I was distressed and bewildered having not seen or encountered any living beings.***

***Then wandering about for a long time in the inundation, O king of men, I was fatigued and did not find shelter anywhere.***

Where did this happen, in the physical or in the astral existence? Did Markandeya perceive this with physical vision? There is mention of the Yaksha nature spirits and the devilish entities on the supernatural plane. At this stage during the dissolution, everything happened on the supernatural level. The physical level was no more as it had retrogressed into its origin which is the unmanifest material energy or psychic stuffs.

# Chapter 5

## Divine Infant

We have to understand that the description of the dissolution which occurred while the creator-god was asleep began as a physical occurrence for Markandeya. It then progressed as a subtle and supernatural occurrence.

Many persons feel that this is all physical. Some think that it is mere myth. However I ask readers to consider this to be mostly supernatural. Markandeya's survival is not a physical one but a supernatural one. Brahmā is not a physical being. Brahmā's deity also, who was seen in an hyper-cosmic divine infant body is a spiritual being.

There will be mention of an extensive banyan fig tree. This tree is more than cosmic, since the whole world system which Brahmā creates fits into the body of the divine infant who will be seen lying on a cosmic leaf which floats by this tree. This tree is larger than our solar system at least.

The fact that we do not experience such vegetation which is larger than the earth even, means that if we are to follow this description we have to shift our comprehension to supernatural possibilities. Markandeya described his meeting with the divine infant to Yudhishthira:

***Once, I saw in the waters of that flood, an enormous, extensive, banyan fig tree, O master of the earth.***

***O king of men, lord of the earth, attached near the end of the branches of this extensive banyan tree there was a bed which was completely covered with a divine bedspread,***

***O King, there sat someone who appeared like the full moon, whose eyes opened like a full blown lotus. Thus I saw a boy, O descendant of the Bharatas.***

This is not physical perception, for that matter it is not the supernatural materials of which our present subtle body consists. It is a supernatural vision which is on par with the vision used by the divine infant.

To see the divine infant, the supernatural water, the supernatural banyan tree and the body of the creator-god Brahmā, one has to have supernatural vision which is on par with the subtlety of those particular dimensions.

Everything which Markandeya perceived in that dimension is non-existent to our sense perception. If such things were before us we could not perceive them. Our scientific instruments would not detect them. To us these are nothing realities, a plane of existence which is never to be perceived by any of the perception means we currently use.

It is interesting that there is a divine tree, growing in divine waters, where there is a divine boy glowing like a full moon. Even in reference to everything there which is on the supernatural plane, the infant glowed noticeably.

Markandeya, the accomplished mystic yogi that he was, who somehow or the other survived the sleeping condition of the deity who produced him, tried to psych the divine infant but his mystic insight made no progress in finding information about the mystery of the child's existence. Who was the child? Where did the infant come from?

***Then, O king of the earth, a great astonishment was felt by me, regarding how this child could exist here despite the destruction of everyone else in the world.***

***By sensually-deprived mystic practice, I psyched him. I had information of the living beings which are to be, but O king of men, I could not penetrate the nature of that child.***

Markandeya as the only survivor of the existential collapse of our world system, including the subtle existence of it, had such deep insight that everyone else in the world except for the creator-god Brahmā was estimated and categorized accurately by him. The divine infant was beyond Markandeya's grasp, being transcendental to the yogi's mystic insight. He described the features of the divine boy:

***Having the complexion of the flax flower, possessing the mark of the special golden curl of hair, he seemed to be the residence of the goddess Lakshmi.***

***Then addressing me, that child whose eyes were like lotus petals, whose form had the special golden curl of hair, who is effulgent spoke words which were pleasing to hear.***

Divine bodies come in varied colors but Krishna's is deep blue, like the color of many flax flowers all crowded together in a field. I saw two of his divine bodies so I know that it is true.

Once I saw one of his four-handed divine bodies, named Padmanabha. Then some years later I saw his Gopala cowherd boy two-handed body, which resembled a juvenile of about 9 years. These were both spiritual bodies. Once when I lived in Minnesota I was surprised when I was travelling along a country road and saw a large field of flax flowers in bloom. The color was exactly the color of the spiritual body of Krishna. Of course those flax flowers are material plants but nevertheless the tone of the deep blue color of an entire 120 acre of blooming flax flowers was the most similar hue to the spiritual body of Krishna.

Later when I used to read the Puranas from India, I found out that the atasī flower was the specified color of Krishna's spiritual body. Atasī is a Sanskrit word for the flax plant. The child spoke to Markandeya.

***(The divine child said:)***

***My dear son, I know that you are thoroughly fatigued. You dearly wish to take rest. O Mārkaṇḍeya, descendant of Bhrigu, you may rest here for as long as you wish.***

***O best of the philosopher-yogis, enter the interior of my body. Live there. O dear one, that is the residence selected by me. I am pleased with you.***

Yogi Markandeya had no idea of the identity or function of the divine boy. The child declared that Markandeya was tired and instructed him to take rest.

Needless to say, the old yogi, the lone survivor from this creation, was puzzled:

***Then O descendant of Bharata, by the influence of that boy, there was a feeling of liberation from material existence and a disgust for material existence in terms of the long life of my body and my existence as a human being.***

The energy of the divine boy abolished Markandeya's basis as a materialistic being. It even subtracted Markandeya's identity as a subtle being from a material cosmos. Markandeya's social basis for existing was all but removed. All that was left was a desire to be with the divine boy.

I actually found this to be true in both of my meetings with the two divine bodies of Krishna which I described before. When one meets him, one loses all interest in one's existence in any other place. One only feels that one needs to be in his association always.

Despite that feeling one may not be allowed to remain with the deity. One might have to return to the existence one endured in a material world or in some other existence, even in the subtle or supernatural world. The deity cannot be commanded to award permanent association.

Everything Markandeya worked to achieve for many years doing yoga austerities, seemed to be no accomplishment, when he felt the influence of that divine child. This is because a yogi must first get a motivation from the material existence itself before he or she can strive for liberation. Everything one does from this end of existence involves being motivated by the very existence one attempts to transcend. Thus it is flawed. But if one is lucky to meet Krishna's divine body, then all phases of energy from the material world are vacated from one's psyche.

In the following verse, Markandeya accredits the divine boy with divine mystic power, such that when the boy opened his mouth, Markandeya was drawn into the infant body:

***Then suddenly that boy opened his mouth. By his divine mystic technique I, who was disempowered, entered him.***

Markandeya was disempowered. The greatest yogi of all, the person who transcended his creator-deity but who was not malicious towards that deity, found his mystic skill to be non-applicable to a mere infant. Still Markandeya only gained more curiosity about the identity and existential function of the deity. This is what happened immediately after:

***Then O king of humanity, having suddenly entered into his abdomen, I saw the entire world with countries and cities.***

***While travelling around I saw the Ganges river, the Shatadru, the Sītā, the Yamunā, the Kauśikī, the Charmanvati, the Vetravati, the Candrabhāgā, the Sarasvati,***

***...the Sindhu and also the Vipāśā river, as well as the Godāvarī, the Vasvokasārā, the Nalini and the Narmada, O descendant of Bharata,***

***...rivers Tāmrā and the sanctifying and fear-producing Veṇṇā, the Suvena and Krishnavena, the Irāmā and Mahānadī, the Śoṇa and O tiger among men, the Viśalyā and Kampuna rivers.***

***I saw those and other rivers on the earth while touring about, O best of human beings. I saw this in the abdomen of that greatest of the souls.***

During the breakdown of the cosmos, as Markandeya knew it, the yogi wondered about the cause of the dissolution as to its whys and wherefores. He was concerned about the wholesale destruction of the creatures, a merciless occurrence in his view.

Now in a boy's body, here was the same world all over again existing as if it was not annihilated. What was this? An illusion? A double creation? Was there a second Markandeya in this creation whom he would meet, his existential double created by a creator-deity or even by the mysterious and spiritually-potent boy?

Markandeya saw more:

***Then O killer of the enemy forces, I saw the ocean, that mine of jewels, the great refuge of water, inhabited by masses of sea monsters.***

***There I saw the sky with the sun and moon, illustrious, blazing with effulgence. The sun was fiery with equal splendor to the sun perceived on the earth before. O king I also saw a vast earth with very beautiful forests.***

***The priestly and tutorial sector of humanity worshiped with many religious ceremonies. The government administrators serviced the other castes with affection.***

The yogi regained his earthly cultural perspective. He repossessed the memory and human psychology when he entered the boy's abdomen. Since he had his wits about him, he compared what he experienced with what he remembered. He found everything to be identical to what was before.

How could this be? How could this boy either preserve the original material world with its possibilities and probabilities or reproduce it exactly, especially since the divine infant was not the person who created these worlds initially. That person was Brahmā who was asleep on the causal plane.

How could this infant maintain the mental creations of that Brahmā Deity, even when those existences had collapsed for a lack of psychological support from the waking consciousness of Brahmā?

The creatures in the original world of which Markandeya was a native, all perished in the global and astronomical cataclysm. Only Markandeya and some super-subtle acquatics survived in a cosmic sea. How then could those physical creatures exist in the boy's gut just as if the destruction of the original creation did not take place.

***The mercantile people did agriculture with skill for the benefit of others. O king, the laborers engaged in rendering service to the duly-trained brahmins.***

***Thus touring around in the abdomen of that Supreme Soul, O king, I saw the Himavat and Hemaketu mountains.***

***I saw the Niṣadha and also the Śveta mountain which has silver ore. I also saw, O king, the Gandhamādana mountain.***

***O tiger among men, I saw the Mandara and the huge Nīla mountain, as well as the gold mountain, Meru,***

***...the Mahendra and the best of mountains, the Vindhya. I also saw the Malaya and the Pāriyātra mountains.***

***These and many others were seen by me in his abdomen, O protector of the earth. All were littered with gems and precious stones.***

The yogi saw natural wonders which were exact replicas of the ones he previously experienced on the earth. This was amazing. Even the smallest details were exactly as it was on the original earth, his native place. People's behavior was the same. Their interaction in trade and labor went on just as in the previous creation.

If an entire cosmos could exist within the boy's body, what was the size of it? Was the boy a physical being, a subtle noumenon, a supernatural or spiritual person?

On which level did the boy exist? How did he derive such existential powers over these creations? Was the whole incidence of the devastated cosmos a superficial occurrence?

The yogi made other observations:

***Lions, tigers, and boars, nāga serpents, O ruler of men, and other living beings on earth, those I saw while travelling around in that master of the world.***

***O tiger among men, having entered his abdomen, I completely toured in all directions. I also saw Śakra Indra and others, the entire hosts of supernatural beings,***

***...the male celestial musicians, the female angelic beings, the Yaksha nature spirits and the enlightened yogis as well, O King. There were clansmen, the rebellious sons of Diti and Danu, the Kāleyas, the leading set of Simhikā's warrior sons, as well as the assigned supernatural rulers and their other opponents.***

Markandeya investigated the subtle material world to be sure that it was the basis for the physical existence which he experienced in the gut of the super-infant. Beneficent supernatural beings from this existence were found to be identical in that world in the body of the boy. There were diabolical magical beings as well, whom if they knew of the boy's existence, might be antagonistic and resistant to him.

Markandeya, the best of the accomplished yogis in Brahmā's world, met the supernatural deities from time to time. Many of them he knew personally. These same beings were alive and well on the particular astral levels where their residences were established. Not one of them appeared to know anything about the destruction of their world which was outside the boy's body; nor were they aware that they existed in a universe which existed within the body of an infant of incredible magical powers.

# Chapter 6

## Yogi is Expelled From the Infant's Body

Markandeya had no control over how he was transited in or out of the divine infant's body. It happened by the mysterious spiritual actions of the divine boy. What else did the boy control? How much leeway did anyone have from the willpower of the infant?

In the infant's body, the yogi maintained vegetarian habits which meant that his psychology and behaviors were not altered in the least, even though his location of existence was changed dimensionally. Markandeya had no way of calculating the distance or existential proximity between the world in the boy's body and the mentally-created world of the Brahmā which perished in the cosmic deluge.

He explained his calculations about the boy's existence:

***Everything in the world was seen by me, all moving and non-moving creatures. I saw it all in the abdomen of that supreme soul. At that time subsisting on fruits, I toured the entire world.***

***Within his body, I existed for hundreds of years. I did not see the end or extent of that body anywhere.***

***Always roving about, investigating and penetrating, O king, I consciously existed but did not find the end to the Supreme Soul.***

This yogi was transferred from the control of the Brahmā deity to the control of the super-infant whose body was discovered to be infinite. Markandeya had no control over it. He lived consciously like a thought in the mind of somebody. Though temporary, a thought exists for a time as a display of awareness.

What materials comprised the boy's body? On what existential support was the boy existent?

Finding no way out of the boy's body, and no one who was perceptible enough to discuss the existence of the boy, Markandeya decided to submit himself to the infant. If anyone understood what existence comprised and how it operated, that person would be the divine boy.

From appearance Markandeya was older than the boy, but existentially, the boy was senior even to the Brahmā deity. In such situations when a yogi reaches the limit of research, when his mystic piercing powers cannot transcend a super-person or a super-realm, then the yogi has no other option but to inquire from a spiritual senior.

***Subsequently, using scriptural procedures, I went to him for shelter. By my actions and intentions I submitted to that distinguished God, the one who bestows blessings.***

Markandeya was lucky to get an immediate response from the deity-infant. Many persons pray to God or to a real or imagined deity and get no response. Markandeya, however, was a special yogi because of his transcendence to the effects of Brahmā's slumber. He explained how he was expelled from the divine infant's body.

In this experience Markandeya did not use a physical body. It may appear as though he did. This is because Markandeya retained the social profile which he had on earth. The body of the boy was not a physical form but since Markandeya was in the dimension in which the boy existed, the boy's body seemed to be of the same energy formation as the yogi's. One amazing detail is in the next verse about the boy's power to either take someone into or expel someone from his divine body.

***Then O king, being thrust by a gust of wind, I was suddenly released through the opened mouth of the Supreme Soul, the Supreme Person.***

***Then O king, tiger among human beings, lying on a branch of the banyan tree, there he was as the Aggregate, the whole world.***

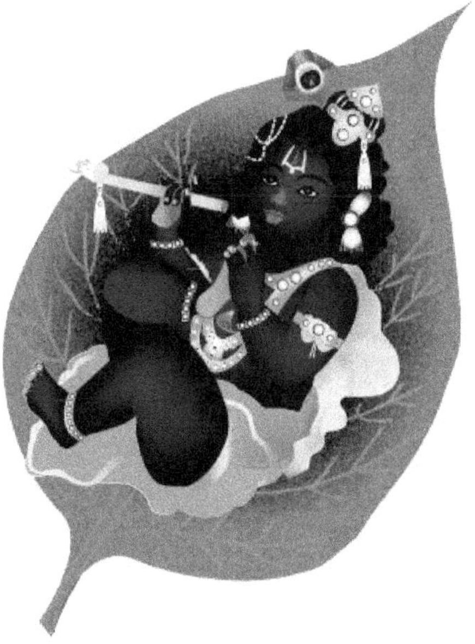

***O tiger among men, I saw him who is beyond measure, the brilliant and effulgent boy who is uniquely marked with the special golden curl of hair.***

The special golden curl of hair, Śrīvatsa, is a feature on the center of the chest of the spiritual bodies of Krishna and His parallel divinities. These deities are known as Vishnu or Narayana (Naa-rai-an-a). No one besides a Vishnu has that mark on the spiritual body.

Markandeya was convinced that this boy was the Aggregate, the whole cosmos. The boy has fabulous powers way beyond anything the yogi considered.

What was the language of the boy? Did the boy use the same speech as Markandeya? Was Markandeya using a body which had a matching expression? Was the communication direct without language transmission?

***Then smiling, the boy, that hero with the special golden curl of hair, the one with shining yellow garments and great effulgence, spoke to me:***

***"O best of the philosopher yogis, Mārkaṇḍeya, for a time you were deep within my body. Listen to what is said by me."***

***Thus from the time that was said to me, a new insight was perceived which provided release from material existence for my spiritual self and a new range of consciousness.***

The sheer presence of the divine boy transited Markandeya to the Absolute. He was released from material existence both psychologically and environmentally. Markandeya experienced a permanent promotion from the mystic level of consciousness he achieved previously when he became proficient in yoga practice on this planet. It happened by the grace of the divine infant. Markandeya now transcended even the consciousness of the creator-deity, Brahmā, who was considered to be the source of Markandeya and everyone else in this creation.

The colors of the supernatural body of the boy were described by the yogi:

***O dear, his copper-colored palms and soles, his very nice well formed feet and beautiful red-colored fingers, have a yellow hue.***

***Having seen his infinite influence and effulgence, with delight, I grasped the two lotus feet while bowing with my head.***

Even though the deity demanded no acclaim and honor, Markandeya with bowed head, fittingly grasped the boy's lotus feet.

***The Soul of all creatures, that God in Person, the one whose eyes are shaped like lotus petals, was seen by me. With joint palms, I approached him eagerly with submission.***

***Having joined palms and offering due worship and attendance with appropriate speech, I said:***

***O God, I wish to know you and also this, your most spectacular creation.***

In such a situation one has no other recourse but to request information. When one reaches the limit of inquiry, when one's perceptive power no longer applies, when one's comprehension fails to come to terms with a reality, one should request an explanation from a higher personality.

How many of these creations did the boy have? Where were they? Did he have others which were not in his supernatural body? How long would he maintain them? Were these systems merely ideas in the spiritual anatomy of the infant?

The yogi made his case to the boy deity:

***Having entered your body through its mouth, O Lord, I saw all the worlds in your abdomen.***

Which worlds did Markandeya purview? Was it a parallel cosmos? How was Markandeya using an existential detachment which only he and the boy experienced?

***O God, existent within your body are the assigned supernatural rulers, the powerful devilish sons of Danu, the ordinary mischievous entities, the Yaksa nature spirits and the nāga serpents, in fact all the stationary and mobile creatures in the world.***

The yogi rightly addressed the infant as Deva or God. This title was fitting. After having such an experience, even the staunchest athiest would agree that the acclaim was fitting.

***Due to your special favor to me, O God, the memory of what was inside you as I wandered everywhere through your body, was not forgotten.***

***O person with the lotus-shaped eyes, I wish to know you, faultless one. Your Lordship, why as a boy do you stay at this place, having swallowed the world? You may explain this if you can.***

Markandeya inquired in the most sensible way. He could not be certain that what happened was not spontaneous. It may be deliberate or non-deliberate. There was no telling if the boy did this impulsively or with intent.

What was the place of the boy's residence? There was a causal plane within the existence of the creator-deity Brahmā. From that place all of Brahmā's creation was produced. Since Brahmā was asleep, his objectivity being shut down, where did the infant exist? Was it within the environment of someone else's mind?

The convention of seniority is the adult stage as in the case of Brahmā. Thus why did this God have an infant form? Was there a mission which this deity served? Was there a rhyme or reason for his actions?

***O dear one, for what purpose is the entire world in your body? Time-wise, how much longer will you stay at this place, O subduer of the rebel souls?***

***I am eager to hear of this, O Lord of the supernatural rulers, for this is suitable information for a brahmin. O lotus-eyed one, explain this in detail, precisely as it developed so that I may be directly linked to this cosmic inconceivable occurrence which I saw in you, O honorable One.***

As a trained accomplished yogi, Markandeya wanted to permanently integrate into his psyche, the experience of the God Infant and the world in the God's body. He wanted to remember it forever. He asked that he should be linked to it from then onwards.

There is a similarity between this experience of Markandeya and the apparition of the Universal Form of Krishna which was shown to Arjuna on the battlefield of Kurukshetra. Arjuna lost contact with the vision later on. He realized that he lost something that was most valuable so he requested of Krishna to bestow the vision once again but Krishna refused.

Markandeya being a seasoned yogi, and realizing that memory of the experience would depend on the grace of the Deity, asked for special recall powers which would keep the experience fresh in memory from then onwards no matter where he would be transited in these creations.

Markandeya, for one reason or the other, was distressed about the cosmic deluge that destroyed the world of which he was a member. This vision of the same world in the infant's body changed his assessment of these cosmic annihilations. Markandeya wanted to maintain contact with the experience so as not to fall back into the same illusory compassion again.

***Thus being addressed by me, that illustrious person, the God of gods, the person who is the greatest effulgence, the endearing one, the best of the speakers, gave this lecture.***

# Chapter 7

## Identity of the Divine Boy

***With satisfaction the deity said:***

***Even the supernatural rulers, O educated mystic priest, do not know details of the truth about me. Being pleased with you however, I will explain how I produce this.***

No matter how great one is, if one is a creation in the mind of another person, then one is limited in reference to that deity. How can we be sure that we are not mere figments of some deity's imagination? The possibility is there even though we may not be able to conclusively prove or disprove it.

If we are figments of someone's visualizations, then there is no way for us to transcend that person, nor could we perceive that person while he or she is in the act of creatively visualizing our existence.

An explanation by the deity was the only way for Markandeya to could understand the process of how the world existed and how its parallel production took place.

***You are devoted to your ancestors, O educated mystic priest, master teacher of mystic yogis. You came for shelter and directly perceived me. You are a great yogi whose sexual energy is neutralized.***

The deity acclaimed Markandeya as someone who appreciated the services performed previously by the ancestors and who took into account the seniority of the ancestors, even though their credits were for the most part, social assets. There is a God of each of these creations wherever they may be. Even though people cannot perceive the divine authority, they do cry out to the deity, who appreciates anyone who does not harass others unfairly.

Markandeya realized his spiritual gender and did not focus on its sexual application. Thus he was not a nuisance in the creation. The deity appreciated the yogi. When gender evolves into sexual expression, complexities arise due to the need for specialized private relationships with various entities. These social complications create undue selfishness and hostility. The deity appreciated that Markandeya had removed himself from the realm of sexuality and remained in the balanced state of gender differentiation only.

The deity explained his habitat and name:

***I named the water Nārā. Due to that, I was identified as Nārāyaṇa, since it was always my habitat or ayana.***

***I am the one called Nārāyaṇa, the existential reality, the eternal, the indestructible principle, the producer of all things and ultimate destroyer, O best of the qualified ritualists.***

Nārāyaṇa is pronounced Naa-rai-an-a. It means the person who lives on the Causal Ocean. The value of the world varies from person to person. It varies considerably from one of its creatures to its producer. An idea can hardly have an inkling about its conceiver.

The deity explained how he could be perceived through his presence as Vishnu or through his influence which empowers powerful entities:

***I am the God Vishnu. I am present in Procreator Brahmā, in Śakra Indra, who is the chief official among the supernatural rulers. I am there in King Vaiśravaṇa Kubera, as well as in Yama, the deity for the disembodied spirits.***

***I am present as Shiva, Soma, Kashyapa, and as the primal progenitor. I am there as Dhātā and Vidhātā. I am the***

***effective religious ceremony in person. O best of the brahmins.***

Vishnu is the form of the deity who produces Brahmā, who is merely a creator-agent. Śakra Indra is the person in the celestial world, who acts as the chief official of the minor deities. These authorities have subtle jurisdiction over many living entities in the material and astral worlds.

King Vaiśravaṇa Kubera is supposed to control the distribution and discovery of natural resources, which are always a source of contention for exploitive entities. Yama is the deity who directs the disembodied spirits in the afterlife, He manages their entry into particular species and families in the next life.

Shiva is regarded as the god of destruction, the merciless terminator of whatever was created by Brahmā. Soma is the deity of moonlight. Kashyapa is one of the primal progenitors who serve the deity by generating human and non-human progeny. Dhātā and Vidhātā are two of the twelve sons of a celestial woman named Aditi. They are regarded as supernatural controllers.

The divine child said that he was any effective religious ceremony in person. Religion really means to recognize and honor of the Supreme Person. The boy identified himself with the altar of the deity in certain Vedic ceremonies:

***Many hundreds of sacrifices were respectfully and skillfully completed with appropriate gifts by me. The expert knowers of the Vedas worship me as I am situated as the altar of the deity.***

Vedic worship ceremonies are not all valid. Not every religious ceremony will connect the worshipper with this boy deity. And still many Acharyas, Pundits, spiritual Masters, leaders of disciplic lineages and brahmins declare to the world and to their followers, that they are in touch with the deity and that whatever they do is consistent with the requirements for worshipping this deity Nārāyaṇa, God Vishnu.

In the time of Markandeya, the deity himself claimed identity with the ceremonies and the altar where the items of the ceremony were placed.

***Rulers on earth who aspire to be like Indra, who are eager to attain the heavenly world, worship me, and so do the business class who are anxious to be transferred to the celestial places.***

Indra is the official who presides over the lower deities. Politicians, who desire to go to a heavenly world after death, must get the approval of this Indra deity. When a politician behaves in a way which is admired by Indra, the deity facilitates his transition to a heavenly world after death. In that dimension, Indra gives hints to the politicians about how to act on earth so as to become a permanent resident of a heavenly world.

Business people who share wealth with the masses and who set an example with grand religious ceremonies in which God is glorified and many poor people are catered and fed, develop in their auras, an affinity to the Indra deity. Thus after death, they transit to a celestial world for a time, depending on the effect-energy of their pious activities.

***Becoming Śeṣa, the supernatural serpent, I support the earth which is bounded by the four seas and studded with the Meru and Mandara mountains.***

***O educated one, long ago, assuming the form of Vārāha the boar, I dove into the cosmic water and courageously lifted this world out of it.***

***Becoming the fire from the mouth of the horse constellation, I, O best of the duly-trained brahmins, drank the water and it is I who agitated and created everything again.***

In the Vedic pantheon of deities, Śeṣa is a supernatural serpent, who is rated as a divine being. In the physical world we find many species of life with the human being as the most versatile. In the subtle dimensions which are not the spiritual world, there are also varied species of life. These are realized in astral projections and can be verified to anyone who becomes aware of astral activity when the astral body is separated from the physical form, during sleep.

The spiritual world is neither this physical existence nor the astral dimensions. It has to be experienced separately in a spiritual body which is not the astral body we use in astral projections and dreams. In the spiritual world, there are varied species, all of which are 100% transcendental.

Meru and Mandara are mountain ranges which were prominent at the time Markandeya had this experience with the deity. Vārāha is the boar incarnation of the Supreme Being. There is a story about this deity, who lifted the earth out of a cosmic deluge in the past. Similar pastimes are enacted in other cosmic floods.

The floods are subtle phenomena which might be compared to physical catastrophes. One may develop confidence in this information through astral projections where one finds that in the astral world there is good weather and bad weather. There is climate in the astral world. The catastrophes which take place there are fantastic in comparison to what we experience on earth.

Constellations sometimes eat one another, just as large fish or very aggressive small fish may successfully devour other aquatics. On one plane of existence there are deities monitoring the development of galaxies. Sometimes there is an attack of one deity to another. This cosmic violence involves supernatural forces.

Just as Markandeya was swallowed by the divine child, and it was not a violent act but an opportunity for education and research for the yogi, so some seemingly-catastrophic astronomical events are devoid of violent intent on the supernatural or spiritual planes but are interpretive of it on the physical level.

The deity attributed a connection between the four primary employment tendencies and the functions of various parts of his body:

***From my mouth, brahmins; from my arms, the political administrators; from my thighs, the mercantile sector of humanity; from my feet, the laborers were produced, in sequence.***

This may be regarded as a supernatural segregation between the various castes or classes of humanity. It is not intended for abuse but it comes under scrutiny because human beings are receptive to both animal instinct and divine influence. From animalism we derive predatory tendencies which promote exploitation.

We are pulled in two opposing directions; up to the divine or down into the animalism. Over time, an individual realizes this and turns away from the vicious way of life.

***The Rig, Sama, Yajur and Atharva Vedas are manifested from me. These enter into me as well.***

The Vedas have spiritual as well as material knowledge. These literatures have survival instructions. This is because the Vedas were given to ancient humans who had to survive under primitive circumstances. Some of the Vedas are not suitable for spiritual cultivation. To correct this information, Krishna culled the spiritual content and gave that as the Bhagavad Gita. In the period of the Upanishads, some effort was made by advanced yogis to partition the transcendental content of the Vedas.

Ultimately this existence digresses into causal energy and enters into the supernatural body of the divine boy who spoke to Markandeya.

# Chapter 8

## Yogis Who Worship the Divine Infant

This boy deity gave an assessment and appreciation of the great yogis. There are many types of yogis with many objectives; some good, some bad. This appraisal regards the yogis who become successful with good motivations:

***The yogis, those who have the supreme spiritual peace, those who are disciplined in soul consciousness, those who are eagerly seeking liberation, those who are free from lust, anger and envy, those who are distant from social associations, those who are psychologically uncontaminated,***

***...those who are situated in psychic clarity, those without a misplaced sense of identity, those whose core-selves are centered on the eternal, those educated brahmins worship me with meditative focus.***

Meditative focus is mastered in the samyama practice which is defined by Patanjali as being a three-part sequential development, beginning with linking one's refined attention to a higher plane of reality, either to another environment or to a deity who is on a transcendental level.

Once the linkage is attained, it may become effortless, meaning that the meditator does not have to exert to maintain it. Once it becomes spontaneous, requiring no effort, it may be sustained for a period of say twenty minutes, half of an hour or more. This sequence is called samyama.

There are different classes of yogis assessed by the deity.

## Yogis who have the supreme spiritual peace

*These yogis, who come to terms with material existence, are evolved sufficiently through the mundane evolutionary cycle to appreciate it for what it is but to also know that it is undesirable. Even though the material world benefits the limited entity, it subjects the entity to unpleasant returns which may throw the entity into confusion and mental darkness. That is Nature's undesirable feature.*

*The supreme peace is psychological and social. Some yogis are psychologically resolved and they let the matter of spiritual research end there. They feel no need for a spiritual social environment. After detaching themselves from the mundane evolutionary cycle, they become so fulfilled in spatial existence even without objectivity, that they stop participating in the opportunities which Nature offers them.*

*Other yogis strive further to meet persons in the spiritual world. Markandeya was such a yogi, who wanted to be in an environment where he could meet the deity, converse with that divine person and understand how God produces the world.*

## Yogis who are disciplined in soul consciousness

*These yogis were desperate to realize their individual spiritual selves without respect to the psychic adjuncts which seem to make up the identity of the self when it is involved in the material world. Self realization really means to discover the spiritual self, in its neutral identity and to barricade the core-self from the various psychic adjuncts which influence it.*

*This kind of person is disciplined in soul consciousness to such an extent that he or she becomes oblivious of time, space and movement.*

*To live in this state perpetually, one should practice meditation wherein one isolates the core self from its adjuncts, like the kundalini life force and the intellect. If the core-self could realize itself in distinction from the psychic accessories, then it may discover if it can exist without the adjuncts. This information would empower it, to retract its reliance on the psychic orbs.*

## Yogis who are eagerly seeking liberation

*Yogis who are eager for liberation and who are realistic, pose no trouble to any other living entities. This is appreciated by the*

*Supreme Being. Even if a yogi has no experience with a Supreme Person, even if he or she only attests to a supreme force, a Primal Creative Cause, still if the yogi is realistic he or she will create no bothersome situation for other living entities. Subsequently the ascetic will have a relatively trouble-free existence wherever he or she may be in these creations.*

*No matter what a limited living entity may do or say, still it is not supreme. It cannot create its environment out of nothing. It has to find a domain which already exists or it may create a territory out of something which is already a reality-energy. This means that in all respects one has to confirm to some expression of reality.*

*The social value of seeking liberation is that it frees a specific entity from the complex organism which becomes manifest to us as history of a particular dimension. When even one entity is freed from that there is a release of tension in the organism of fate. That is appreciated by the Supreme Being, even if the said yogi is not interested in a relationship with the deity. This does not happen however if the yogi is ill-motivated, in which case he or she does not become liberated but instead becomes a source of increased stress in the layout of providence.*

## Yogis who are free from lust, anger and envy

*Yogis who are free from lust, anger and envy, are usually still involved in the material world. They act as saviors and social reformers. These persons are interested in grand harmonies in realms which cannot become harmonious through and through.*
*The result of their work is that one or two entities leave aside the life of exploitation and develop qualities which are becoming of an elevated soul.*
*The teacher-yogis who are free from lust, anger and envy and who focus on creating harmony among human beings, do not perform the terminal austerities which are required for elevation out of the material world.*
*Still, their endeavor is appreciated by the Supreme Being because it acts as a conduit for his compassion. Eventually, these yogis see that their effort to create utopia is an idea only. This world remains as it is because of the quality of its inherent energy.*

## Yogis who are distant from social associations

*In contrast to those yogis who work for world harmony, there are yogis who move away from human society. They are allergic to human association. They prefer to live in isolation. This effort results in the benefit of rapid assessment of the yogi's existence, view of other dimensions and contact with disembodied advanced entities. Such yogis also derive inspiration from the Supreme Person.*

*Persons who are detached by nature, and who do not care one hoot about social development, become yogis without social missions. People feel that they are anti-social and indifferent but their situation is one of aversion to being under the dominance of material nature.*

*Mere aversion however, does not free anyone from nature's control. This is why these yogis go to a remote place and take up austerities to wean themselves from the advantages they derived from nature.*

*When a living entity gives up reliance on one nature, it will still be required to take refuge somewhere else. Reliance, once it is experienced, indicates that it is a permanent feature of that particular soul. Thus it is a matter of switching to the spiritual plane and taking shelter there.*

*The Supreme Person, Krishna, will automatically assist any living entity who performs sufficient austerity which qualifies that person for an exit from material existence. Thus these yogis get divine grace which reinforces their endeavors and make them successful in the bid to transit to the spiritual places.*

## Yogis who are psychologically uncontaminated

*There is atma yoga. This is inward focus on the core-self in meditation. There is a similar discipline which is called kriya yoga. Both of these are inter-related. In fact some of the practices of atma yoga are identical to some in kriya yoga. What then is the difference?*

*Atma yoga is for persons who are disinclined from having a psychic body. Kriya yoga is for those who realize that a psychic body is a must in the subtle and gross material worlds. If one has a strong dislike for a psychic body, one will select atma yoga as the path of spiritual life. In that practice, the focus is the core-self alone. It is not concerned with the psychic adjuncts like the sense of identity, intellect, life force, subtle senses and memory. In Patanjali yoga, everything having to do with the adjuncts is shut down.*

*However to be realistic one has to understand that unless one becomes very powerful and supremely detached, it will not be possible to get rid of the adjuncts. A belief in theory of atma yoga or kriya yoga does not empower anyone to shut down the adjuncts. Only austerity renders for the individual the power to curtain and eventually squeeze out the influence of the psychic organs which usually compel the self to operate a spiritually non-productive lifestyle.*

*Patanjali, even though he instructed the yogis to scrap the adjuncts, to silence them once and for all, did in the last chapter of the Yoga Sutras suggest that at first one has to isolate the core-self (atma) from the adjuncts. When the adjuncts become purified or neutralized, the yogi may be again fused with them in their purified non-destructive state.*

*This means that the atma or core-self will have to keep the adjuncts but it has the responsibility for purifying and controlling these psychic accessories.*

## Yogis who are situated in psychic clarity

*Yogis who are situated in psychic clarity are persons who began doing yoga with some psychic perception. Many persons come to yoga without any psychic insight. It may be said that such students begin the practice with a psychically blind and deaf psyche. After hearing about yogis who have clairvoyant powers, these students develop a desire to attain mystic perception. Some are successful. Some are not.*

*Psychic clarity is useful in yoga in the area of getting assistance from departed siddha yogis who are on higher planes of existence. One has a great advantage if one has accurate psychic perception, since by that one can take instructions in the subtle world from the siddhas.*

## Yogis without a misplaced sense of identity

*Those yogis who are without misplaced sense of identity are special personalities who are rated as empowered incarnations of divinity. They serve the mission for which they took a body and do not get involved in social activities which are excessive.*

*Since they do not misuse identity, they do not struggle to control the expression of* ***I*** *and the grasping feature of* **mine***. They also do not have a misconception whereby they feel that all identity is troublesome and should be scrapped.*

*Each limited spirit is to an extent an identity unto itself but that declaration is valid only within the framework of the overarching reality. The self cannot get rid of its core-identity. The troublesome applications of identity should be terminated, not the identity sense itself. For that matter the sense of identity cannot be eliminated.*

## Yogis whose core-selves are centered on the eternal

*These are the yogis who manage to focus on causal principles. They do this instinctively. This gives them the advantage of minimum investment of energy into the gross material existence.*

*These are called sat yogis or ascetic beings who focus on reality. By convention human beings focus on material existence. They are mostly oblivious of the activities of the subtle body which is fused into the physical one and which will separate from that one permanently at death.*

*Sat yogis are involved in the subtle substrata of the material world. They are criticized for not giving sufficient value to the material body and its associations.*

The boy deity identified himself with the sun and the luminaries:

***I am the solar flare. I am the light of the flare. I am supervisor of death from the solar flare. I am the sun itself, the cosmic flare. I am the air which comprises the solar flare.***

***Regarding the forms of the stars perceived in the sky, know these as being my forms, O best of the duly-qualified mystic priests.***

One way to consider this is to conceive that everything is the expression of personality. Personality pervades everything seen or unseen. We have a hang-up where we feel that unless we see a living gross form, we are not dealing with personality. In fact some of us think that only a live human form is expressive of personality.

One has to transcend this natural prejudice. Consciousness itself is not restricted to living forms. The truth is that we cannot account fully for personality. We simply cannot identify all the forms of it, or the expressive influences of it. This is because we have limited sense perception. The divine boy advised the yogi to consider the stars as forms of the deity. Even minerals were rated as affiliate possessions of the divine child:

***The mines of precious stones and the oceans, as well as the four cardinal points, know these as my garments, resting place and residence.***

# Chapter 9

## Actions of the Divine Infant

In a creation like this, one has to account for negative aspects. Production, duration and demolition are the three phases of whatever becomes manifest grossly in the material world. Thus any consideration which does not include those stages is incomplete.

Whatever is manifested indirectly, whatever is just indicated here, escapes from scrutiny due to its transcendental feature. Addressing the yogi as the best of the reality-perceivers, the divine child explained that negative emotions are forms of his energy:

***Craving, violent disappointment, pleasure, fear and even delusion, know that these too are my forms, O best of the reality-perceivers.***

The boy explained that the positive aspects are regulated by him only:

***O educated brahmin, whatever people achieve through socially-beneficial activity, realistic living, charity, austerity and extreme non-violence towards all living beings,***

***...they get by my allowance. Their pastimes are enacted within my body as supervised by me. They perform not by their desire and will but as accommodated by me.***

Does he do this voluntarily or involuntarily, deliberately or impulsively, spontaneously or after much planning?

He explained that the desire and will of everyone else was within the confines of his supervision and what happens is only permissible under his autonomy.

***Those who have thoroughly studied the Vedas, those who are spiritually-satisfied, those who conquered anger, those duly-qualified ritual priests are rewarded through the performance of various kinds of approved religious ceremonies.***

In the time of Markandeya, duly qualified ritual priests consummated their studies (Vedas), their introspection and self-control by performing approved religious ceremonies. Everything was finalized by an appropriate religious ceremony in which a deity was invoked.

They recognized more than one deity. They also recognized that the Supreme Person delegated authority to other regulators. For trivial items they consulted with a minor deity. For events of significance they reached higher deities or the Supreme Person.

In private yoga practice, this is also done, except that it may be performed on a subtle plane. The situation of Markandeya serves the sample, showing that during the devastation, he could not service even approved religious acts,. Mentally however he remained true to the cause of spiritual relationship and did not disrespect nor try to surpass Brahmā the creator-deity. Later of course Markandeya met the divine child, the supervisor of Brahmā.

That sequence of events is remarkable and hard to comprehend because there was no explanation of how Markandeya was shifted from the devastation to the place where the boy resided near the supra-cosmic banyan tree.

When Brahmā fell asleep everything in these worlds collapsed. The forms were denied their various configurations. There was just cosmic water with Brahmā and Markandeya.

Brahmā's body was sleeping thereafter. The divine boy and Markandeya were awake. But where were they located? What dimension were they in? Where is that place in relation to our situation?

What was the world in the boy's body which Markandeya found to be identical to the one which Brahmā created but which collapsed when Brahmā's objective consciousness faded?

The deity explained the undesirable situation of persons who are prone to faulty acts:

***Know that this is not possible for men who perform faulty or criminal acts, or who render no beneficial social service, or who have not subdued the impulse for greed, or who are without mercy, without culture of the spiritual self.***

He contrasted this to those who perform approved acts which are beneficial to one and all:

***Know from me about the great benefits and position of one whose social activities are done nicely. O educated brahmin, that is not acquired by those who are foolish. The yogis engage in the proper method.***

One must have insight, intuition or reliable information to know how to act in a way which yields positive results in the long term. A yogi is not concerned with accrued benefits but since he or she must act, it is decisive to act for the benefit of one and all.

This creation is a repository of resentments. If a yogi has to appear in it today or tomorrow, he should never forget the content of this place. There is no sense in acting the fool and then being subjected to adverse consequences in the future.

When resentments build up to an explosive point, the Supreme Being may act to relieve the situation. He may deal with it directly or he may do so through an agent or agency:

***Whenever there is a decrease of the righteous lifestyle, O best of the reality-perceivers, and an increase in the inappropriate behavior, then I make a personal appearance.***

***When the rebellious sons of Diti, who crave violence and who are resistant to being killed even by the best of the duly appointed supernatural rulers, as well as the ordinary mischievous entities, roam on this earth, being formidable and challenging,***

***...I appear in families which are productive of auspicious cultural activities. Assuming a human body, I pacify everyone.***

***Having created the supernatural rulers, the human race, the celestial musicians, the uraga serpents, the mischievous sub-humans, I, by mystic magic completely annihilate the stationary and mobile living beings.***

***In the time of such situations, I repeatedly consider and create for myself a body, coming as a human being for the purpose of establishing the boundaries of morality.***

Even though the spiritual infant produces a body for himself on a lower plane, the assumption of life on that level does not detract from his divine status. His native forms are spiritual. Those are eternal. He also produces other forms which are temporal.

It is natural that if one meets a divine being on a lower level, one would assume that he or she is just as fallible as anyone else. Which imagined being in someone's mind could rightly assess the category of the thinker if that creator entered into the plane of the imagination?

Our proneness to assessing everything within our sense perception as being no greater than ourselves, as well as the situational limitations which prevent us from transcending physical existence, are natural.

The divine child gave a schedule of his entry into the earth plane from time to time. Nothing changes on the transcendental level for the infant even if he assumes a human form or even an animal form on a lower plane. He is not limited to being just a divine being. He can descend into a lower level. He can assume or operate a body on the physical plane. None of these acts erases or lowers his existential autonomy.

***In the Era of Easy Achievement, I appear with a white complexion. In the Tretā Third Era, I have a yellow color. In the Era of the devilish deity, Dvāpara, I assume a red hue. In the Era of the Devil Kali, I have a blackish tone.***

***Moreover, in time there is a three part (out of four) portion of the socially-destructive lifestyles. At that time, the occasion develops, so I, alone, as death personified, destroy the entire three sectors of this existential situation, which consist of mobile and immobile beings.***

The Tretā Era is the third in sequence but when there is an irregularity in time, it appears as the second era. Time is usually linear, but periodically there are jumps in time which cause irregularity.

In the last era, which is named after the devilish supernatural being Kali, there is a three-fourths portion of socially-destructive lifestyles. The divine boy is aware of the moral situation of humanity. From time to time, he acts to boost righteous lifestyle or to destroy socially-degrading behavior. He explained his transcendence in this way:

***I am the one who covers everything in three steps; the soul of all beings, the person who is all the worlds. I give happiness. I am the Primary Person in these worlds. I***

***penetrate all. I am endless. I am the Lord of the senses. I cross all boundaries.***

This being is the exception, the ultimate transcendence, the unfathomable person, beyond all calculations, intuitions and perceptions. He is God!

***O brahmin, I, alone, set the cycle of time into motion. I am formless. Indeed, I am the destroyer of all creatures. I am the motivator of all the worlds.***

The formless condition of this being relates to his spiritual body being out of reach of the senses of anyone. This being is the container of all and cannot be contained by anyone. He is the ultimate person-dimension:

***Thus ascertained, O best of the philosopher yogis, all beings are penetrated by me but no one knows me, O leader of the educated brahmins.***

***Whatever psychological trauma you endured within my body, O duly-trained brahmin, was for the increase of your happiness and well-being, O faultless one.***

Markandeya was curious about the source of creation. He qualified himself for the research by thorough austerities. Thus the deity gave objective proof of the situation. The deity promoted the existential energy of Markandeya, even to a level beyond that of the Brahmā. And still, we find that Markandeya respected Brahmā as being superior. Markandeya is an exemplary yogi.

The hardship Markandeya endured while in Brahmā's creation and then the rigors of the existence within the body of the divine infant, were due to Markandeya's persistent curiosity about the primal creative cause. He got the evidence he desired but it included much psychological trauma. The deity reminded the yogi that it was due to desire and persistence to know, that the experiences were awarded.

The deity did not desire to inflict the hardships and survival trials. It was due to Markandeya's prying nature. All other entities did not go through the devastation. They were spared the experience of it as their existences were temporarily cancelled but since the great yogin was curious and performed related austerity, he was allowed a wider span of objective consciousness through which he survived while all others became subjective existences without objective awareness.

The deity declared autonomy over everything everywhere:

***Whatever was seen by you in this world of mobile and immobile creatures was in all respects, established by me, who is the self of it all, O best of the philosopher yogis.***

This is not a general self. This is the individual self of the divine infant. He is not speaking metaphorically or symbolically. This is no allegory. He directly meant himself only.

***The great grandfather of all these worlds is half of my body. I am known as God Nārāyaṇa, the one who holds the conch, disc and club.***

The great grandfather of these worlds is Brahmā, the creator-god. He is an agent of the spiritual infant. When seen in an adult spiritual body with four arms carrying the conch, disc, club and flower, this Supreme Person, the infant, who has multiple parallel divine forms, is known as God Nārāyaṇa.

The existential status of Brahmā's creation in reference to the consciousness of the divine infant was explained in this way:

***O accomplished philosopher-yogi, for as long as the period of one thousand of the four eras persists, so long I, who am the soul of the universe, the great grandfather of all the worlds, sleep while everyone else is transformed into unconsciousness.***

This explains that the material creation and its subtle counterpart shut down for a very long time, for an eternity by our present time constraints. During that period, Brahmā and all other entities, except the divine infant, experience a total loss of awareness.

It is a loss of objective consciousness only but to the objective mind it is total non-existence, a termination of consciousness. The individual souls continue existing as subjective reality only. Their self-knowing abilities are suspended.

The individual spirit is more than its subjective self and yet, it fails to realize itself when it is shifted into subjective awareness alone. This shifting system is controlled by the divine infant, the Supreme Personality.

Markandeya wondered why the divinity was a child's form. The deity explained:

***Thus O best of the philosopher-yogis, I exist here for all time. Though not a child, I assume the form of a child for as long as the deity Brahmā does not become aware.***

The deity did not explain why he had the child form. He only said that his infant form existed at that location during Brahmā's slumber. I thought of asking the Deity for the direct cause of this infant form but then I figured that if the Deity wanted to give the information, he would have given it to Markandeya, one of the greatest siddhas of all time, a perfected yogi, whose reputation rivals even that of his yoga-deity who is Lord Shiva.

Does the deity assume another form when Brahmā awakens? If so, what is that divine form? Are these forms eternal and simultaneously existing?

The activation of the self's objectivity is dependent on the waking state of this divine boy. But the matter does not end there because there is a transcendental transformer existing as the person of Brahmā; such that when he sleeps, they lose objective awareness. They do so even if the divine boy remains awake. Markandeya and the infant were the only beings who transcended Brahmā's waking consciousness.

Brahmā in turn is dependent on the boy's consciousness. So long as the boy is awake, Brahmā may rise, act and then sleep repeatedly but once the boy slumbers, Brahmā's objectivity is finished.

The deity blessed the great yogin:

***O educated brahmin, blessings were repeatedly given to you by me who is the form of exclusive spiritual existence. I am completely satisfied by you, O brahmin. You are a person who is worshipped by groups of accomplished philosopher-yogis.***

Markandeya is worthy of respect from all other yogis. He is a deity of yogis. Anyone who can survive Brahmā's slumber is worthy of the respect given to that creator-deity.

Though he does not require it and never demanded it, Markandeya is worthy of veneration.

***Seeing everything as one vast ocean, with all the mobile and immobile creatures wasted, you were distressed. This was known to me. Thus you were shown that the world still existed (within my body).***

***Entering the inside of my body, you were astonished. Having seen everything in the world there; you became astonished and did not thoroughly understand.***

## Apparition of the Boy Krishna Deity

*After translating this verse, the author had an appearance of this Boy Krishna Deity which Markandeya saw. This happened on the morning of December 3rd 2011, on a Saturday morning while I sat to meditate on a couch at the home of Bharat Patel in Mobile, Alabama.*

*I was just about to finish the meditation session when I had this feeling to stay on and meditate more. In fact on that morning I was late for meditation, some two hours late, but still I felt compelled to meditate just a little more.*

*As soon as I decided to do that, there was a pressure from the back of the head and the naad sound moved forward and I become aware of it. Then a subtle hand held a finger of mine and drew tilak markings on a forehead. This was a Vaishnava marking but it was a bit different to the one I was introduced to by the disciples of Srila Bhaktivedanta Swami Prabhupada. The tilak was like this:*

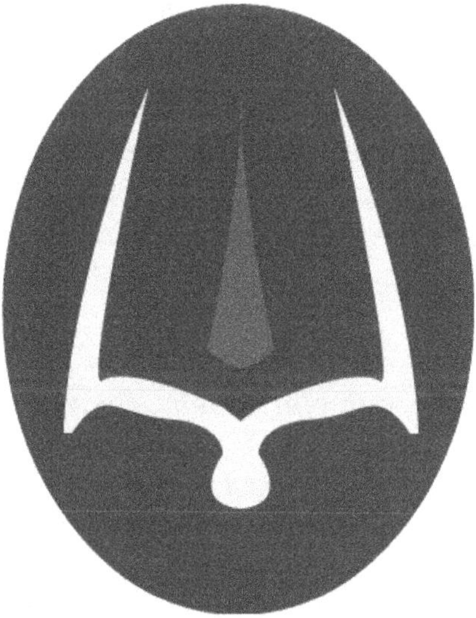

*The hand that held my finger to draw this was the hand of the Deity. He said,*

> ***"Be sure to draw that tilak like this on both the Maharishi's and My illustrations."***

*I could feel the existence of the deity but I could not see his body because it was transparent emanating transparent light. He then said,*

> ***"Is there anything I can do for you? Ask a favor, son."***

*I ran through my mind in a hurry because I felt pressed for time, as if I had to come up with some request quickly before the Deity would disappear. I found no desire in my mind which was blank. I then turned towards my meditation practice and something came to me for requesting of the Deity. I said to him, the Boy Krishna,*

> ***"Help me with this meditation. I need to reach the chit akasha more frequently. If there is something you can instruct, then please reveal that kriya to me."***

*He said,*

> ***"That is strange because you are already in touch with chit akash. Anyway, do this and go here."***

*Then he left.*

*The instruction 'to do this and go here', was an instruction for me to jump up into the high part of the subtle forehead and then to put my attention forward just a little without having the attention go outside the forehead. This causes the membrane of the subtle head to break down, to dissolve and it allows the yogi to make contact with the chit akash.*

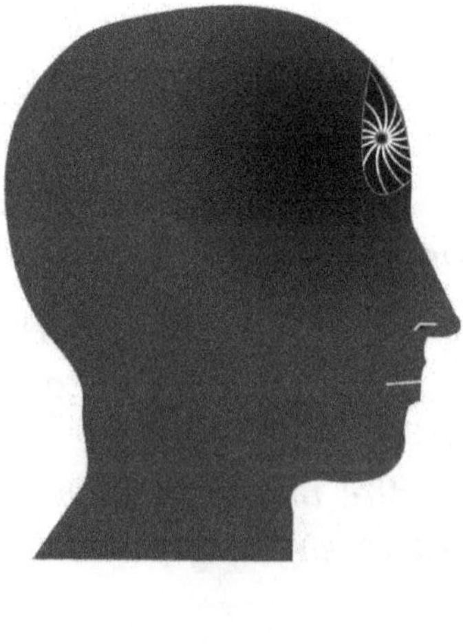

*This is a very simple kriya and it works, however there is a preliminary requirement that the yogi be proficient in breath infusion and kundalini pull-up kriya.*

*There was a notation which the Deity left in my psyche about this particular tilak mark where he said:*

> ***"They do not have use for this. They are not yogis. They feel yoga is useless. In this tilak the space is where the yogi makes contact with the chit akash. This is not just a mark. This is a meditation process.***
>
> ***"Mark it externally or do not mark it externally. But that is not it. It has to do with contact with chit akash. It is the unseen mystic mark in the psyche of the accomplished yogi. What have they to do with this?***
>
> ***"They believe in external physical contact with the deity. They have no confidence in this. Be blessed to continue this, my son."***

# Chapter 10

## Krishna Verified

***Then, O accomplished philosopher-yogi, you were quickly expelled through my mouth. I explained about that special self, who is difficult to ascertain even for the assigned supernatural rulers and the sorcerers who oppose them.***

***While he, the lordly deity, the one with the greatest mystic austerities to his credit, Procreator Brahmā, is not conscious, you can, O accomplished philosopher-yogi, stay here with confidence and happiness.***

This clarifies that there is a serious side to the divine boy. He was not an innocent kid. He was not a human child. The divine form was that of the child but the person who was the form, exhibited mature consideration.

The deity warned Markandeya that the allowance for him to be objectively conscious while Brahmā slept, would end as soon as Brahmā would awaken.

Markandeya would then resume the existential dependence on Brahmā's waking state. This transcendence of Brahmā's consciousness would not be supported forever by the deity. Markandeya would have to resume his existence as a being under the existential jurisdiction of Brahmā.

In the next verse some vital information is given:

***Then when that grandsire of all the worlds, becomes conscious, I will create the host of living beings from my body, O best of the duly-trained mystic priests.***

From our perspective, this verse has vital information about how we are existentially maintained. This gives us some idea of the importance and lack of significance of the Brahmā, the creative overlord, the person in whose mind, we exist.

Though a god in his own right, Brahmā is merely an agent of this divine child. For that matter Brahmā's creative endeavors are underwritten by the child. The beings who perish in Brahmā's world are collectively transferred into the divine body of the boy when Brahmā sleeps and his psyche fails to support our existences any longer.

When Brahmā awakens, the boy transfers the beings into Brahmā's psyche. Then Brahmā produces them in the subtle and physical realities as individual entities with particular lifestyles.

If Markandeya had any ideas about becoming a creator-deity like Brahmā, the boy seemed disinclined to that desire. The great yogi had to resume his existence in Brahmā's mind just as before:

***There will be the sky, the earth, the light, the wind, the water even and everything else for this world, all the mobile and immobile creatures.***

***Mārkaṇḍeya said:***

***O dear one, having said that, the God, the greatest, most spectacular living being, became invisible. I saw these beings, this variegated infinitely-dispersed creation, existing again.***

I can vouch for this type of experience, where one has a visitation by a diving being or one finds oneself in the presence of such a divinity in the chit akash, the spiritual lands. Then the experience abruptly ends, and one can do nothing to repeat the perception.

***This was seen by me O king. At the end of the era, I experienced that wonder, O best of the Bharatas, best of all those who support the virtuous lifestyle.***

*That God who was seen by me long long ago, the person with the eyes like lotus petals, is your family member, Janārdana Krishna, the motivator of people.*

Yogi Markandeya identified Krishna as the divine boy whose existence transcended Brahmā. The yogi realized the privileges granted to him by the divine infant, who is a parallel person of the same Krishna who stood with them during this discourse.

*Due to the boon given to me by this Deity; my memory does not fade; my lifespan is long; death of my body will occur at my convenience.*

*This Krishna, the descendant of Vṛṣṇi, is the Primal Person, the Supreme Person, the one Hari who removes miserable conditions, the inconceivable spirit, the one who plays like a child, the greatest of the multi-taskers.*

*This Krishna is Dhātā and Vidhātā. He is the complete destroyer, a relative of the Sātvata family. He has the Śrīvatsa golden curl of hair on his chest. He is Govinda, the father of the father of the living beings, the master.*

*Having seen this Krishna, the leader of the Vṛṣṇis, my memory surfaced. He is the First and Primary Deity, the Unborn Person, the God Vishnu, the person who wears yellow garments.*

*Krishna, the descendant of Madhu, is the mother and father of all the living beings. Take recourse of this person who is the one a person should rely on, O best of the Kauravas.*

*Vaiśampāyana said:*

*The sons of Pṛthā and the twin who were foremost among the human beings, along with Draupadī, offered respectful homage to Krishna, who was verified as the maintainer of the creatures.*

# Chapter 11

## Mahabharata: Aranyaka (Vana) Parva, Markandeya Samasya, Chapter 187

## Original / Translation

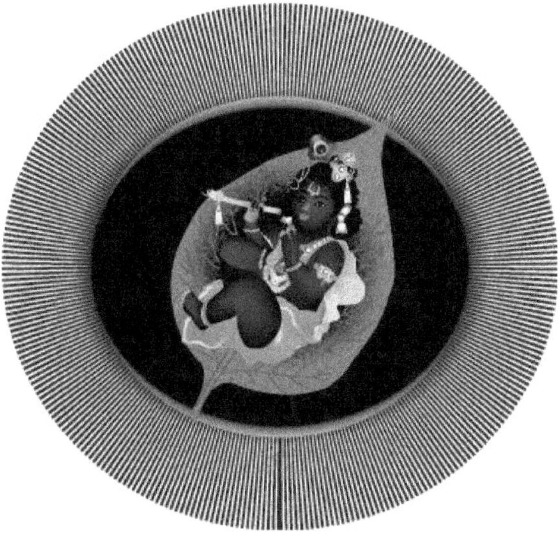

## Verse 1

वैशंपायन उवाच

ततः स पुनरेवाथ मार्कण्डेयं यशस्विनम्

पप्रच्छ विनयोपेतो धर्मराजो युधिष्ठिरः (1.1)

**vaiśaṁpāyana uvāca**
**tataḥ sa punarevātha mārkaṇḍeyaṁ yaśasvinam**
**papraccha vinayopeto dharmarājo yudhiṣṭhiraḥ**

vaiśaṁpāyana - Vaiśaṁpāyana; uvāca – said; tataḥ - then; sa – he; punar = punah = again; evātha = eva (so) + ātha (then); mārkaṇḍeyaṁ - Mārkaṇḍeya; yaśasvinam – celebrated person; papraccha – inquired; vinayopeto = vinayopetah = vinaya (with humility) + upetah (approached); dharmarājo = dharmarājah = king who was righteousness personified; yudhiṣṭhiraḥ - Yudhiṣṭhira

***Then King Yudhiṣṭhira who was righteousness personified, again approached the celebrated Markandeya and inquired with humility.***

## Verse 2

नैके युगसहस्रान्तास्त्वया दृष्टा महामुने

न चापीह समः कश्चिदायुषा तव विद्यते

वर्जयित्वा महात्मानं ब्राह्मणं परमेष्ठिनम् (1.2)

**naike yugasahasrāntāstvayā dṛṣṭā mahāmune**
**na cāpīha samaḥ kaścidāyuṣā tava vidyate**
**varjayitvā mahātmānaṁ brāhmaṇaṁ parameṣṭhinam**

naike = na (no) + eke (in one); yugasahasrāntās = yuga (time cycles) + sahasra (thousands) + antās (antāh.

termnation); tvayā – by you; dṛṣṭā – was seen, witnessed; mahāmune – great yogi-philosopher; na – no; cāpīha = ca (and) + api (also) + iha (here, in this dimension); samaḥ - same, equivalent; kaścid = kaścit = anyone; āyuṣā – longevity; tava – your; vidyate – is knowledgeable, aware; varjayitvā – excluding; mahātmānaṁ - of the Supreme Soul; brāhmaṇaṁ - of deity Brahmā; parameṣṭhinam – of the supremely-intelligent person

***O great yogi–philosopher no one besides you has witnessed the termination of thousands of time cycles. There is no one in this cosmos who is your equivalent in lifespan or who is as knowledgeable, besides the supreme person, deity Brahmā, who is supremely intelligent.***

## Verse 3

अनन्तरिक्षे लोकेऽस्मिन्देवदानववर्जिते

त्वमेव प्रलये विप्र ब्रह्माणमुपतिष्ठसि (1.3)

**anantarikṣe loke'smindevadānavavarjite**
**tvameva pralaye vipra brahmāṇamupatiṣṭhasi**

an – without, not; antarikṣe – in the sky; loke'smin = loke (in the world) + 'smin (asmin, in this)devadānavavarjite = deva (appointed deities) + dānava (sorcerers who oppose the appointed deities) + varjite (being without); tvam – you; eva – even. alone; pralaye – in the cosmic dissolution; vipra – educated mystic; brahmāṇam – of deity Brahmā; upatiṣṭhasi – you attended

***When the world was without sky, without appointed deities and without the sorcerers who oppose the deities, you alone, O educated mystic, attended the deity Brahmā during the cosmic dissolution.***

## Verse 4

प्रलये चापि निर्वृत्ते प्रबुद्धे च पितामहे

त्वमेव सृज्यमानानि भूतानीह प्रपश्यसि (1.4)

**pralaye cāpi nirvṛtte prabuddhe ca pitāmahe**
**tvameva sṛjyamānāni bhūtānīha prapaśyasi**

pralaye – in the cosmic dissolution; cāpi = ca (and) + api (also); nirvṛtte – in the universal dormancy; prabuddhe – in awareness of; ca - and; pitāmahe – in the great cosmic father; tvam – you; eva – only; sṛjyamānāni – in the visualization of the creatures; bhūtān – the living beings; īha – here; prapaśyasi – you perceive

***After the cosmic dissolution reached the stage of universal dormancy, and the great cosmic father became aware, you were the only one who perceived his visualization of the living beings.***

## Verse 5

चतुर्विधानि विप्रर्षे यथावत्परमेष्ठिना

वायुभूता दिशः कृत्वा विक्षिप्यापस्ततस्ततः (1.5)

**caturvidhāni viprarṣe yathāvatparameṣṭhinā**
**vāyubhūtā diśaḥ kṛtvā vikṣipyāpastatastataḥ**

catur = catuh = four; vidhāni - types; viprarṣe = vipra (educated ritual priest) + rṣe (self-realized yogi);

yathāvat – as if, just as well; parameṣṭhinā – by the one who is supremely intelligent; vāyu – air; bhūtā - of elements; diśaḥ -directions; kṛtvā – having done; vikṣipyāpas = vikṣipya (scattering); apas = apah = water; tatastataḥ = then then = there there

***O self-realized yogi who is an educated ritual priest, the four types of beings were produced by the one who is supremely intelligent. Having put the air and elements in all directions, he scattered water here and there.***

## Verse 6

त्वया लोकगुरुः साक्षात्सर्वलोकपितामहः

आराधितो द्विजश्रेष्ठ तत्परेण समाधिना (1.6)

**tvayā lokaguruḥ sākṣātsarvalokapitāmahaḥ**
**ārādhito dvijaśreṣṭha tatpareṇa samādhinā**

tvayā – by you; lokaguruḥ - spiritual master of the world; sākṣāt – from being directly empowered; sarvaloka – all the worlds; pitāmahaḥ- great father of the beings; ārādhito = ārādhitah = devotedly worshipped; dvijaśreṣṭha – best of the initiated ritualists; tat – that; pareṇa – by the highest level of consciousness; samādhinā – by continuous effortless linkage of the attention to a higher concentration force or person

***The spiritual master of the world, the great father of the beings, was directly worshipped by you, O best of the initiated ritualists, by your continuous effortless linkage of attention to the highest level of consciousness.***

## Verse 7

तस्मात्सर्वान्तको मृत्युर्जरा वा देहनाशिनी

न त्वा विशति विप्रर्षे प्रसादात्परमेष्ठिनः (1.7)

**tasmātsarvāntako mṛtyurjarā vā dehanāśinī**
**na tvā viśati viprarṣe prasādātparameṣṭhinaḥ**

tasmāt – therefore; sarvāntako – all ending; mṛtyur = mṛtyuh = death; jarā – old age; vā - or; dehanāśinī – destroyer of the body; na – no; tvā – you; viśati - enters; viprarṣe= vipra (educated ritual priest) + rṣe (self realized yogi); prasādāt – from mercy, grace, favor; parameṣṭhinaḥ - the supremely-intelligent person

***Thus, O self-realized yogi who is an educated ritualist, by the grace of the supremely intelligent person, the termination of everything, death, or old age even, the destruction of all bodies, does not affect you.***

## Verse 8

यदा नैव रविर्नाग्निर्न वायुर्न च चन्द्रमाः

नैवान्तरिक्षं नैवोर्वी शेषं भवति किंचन.(1.8)

**yadā naiva ravirnāgnirna vāyurna ca candramāḥ**
**naivāntarikṣaṁ naivorvī śeṣaṁ bhavati kiṁcana**

yadā – when; naiva – not even; ravir = ravih = sun; nāgnir= na (not) + agnir (agnih, fire); na – not; vāyur = vāyuh = air, gas; na – not; ca – and; candramāḥ - moon; naivāntarikṣaṁ = na (not) + eva (even) + antarikṣaṁ (sky); naivorvī = na(not) + eva (so) + urvī (earth); śeṣaṁ - what remains, end; bhavati – he becomes; kiṁcana – anything, anyone

***When not even the sun, nor fire, nor air, nor the moon, nor even the atmosphere, nor the earth remained;***

## Verse 9

तस्मिन्नेकार्णवे लोके नष्टे स्थावरजङ्गमे

नष्टे देवासुरगणे समुत्सन्नमहोरगे (1.9)

**tasminnekārṇave loke naṣṭe sthāvarajaṅgame**
**naṣṭe devāsuragaṇe samutsannamahorage**

tasmin – in this; nekārṇave = ekārṇave = eka (one) + arṇave (in ocean); loke – in the world; sthāvara – stationary; jaṅgame – moving creatures; naṣṭe – is destroyed; devā – lower deities; suragaṇe – goups of celestial beings; samut - desirous; sanna – motionless, decayed; mahorage = mahā (great) + urage (in the serpents)

***when in this world, there is one ocean, when the stationary and moving creatures were destroyed, as well as the lower deities, the groups of celestial beings and the great serpents become motionless;***

## Verse 10

शयानममितात्मानं पद्मे पद्मनिकेतनम्

त्वमेकः सर्वभूतेशं ब्रह्माणमुपतिष्ठसि (1.10)

**śayānamamitātmānaṁ padme padmaniketanam**
**tvamekaḥ sarvabhūteśaṁ brahmāṇamupatiṣṭhasi**

śayānam – lying down; amitātmānaṁ = amita (boundless, infinite) + ātmānaṁ (self); padme – in the lotus flower; padmaniketanam – person whose residence is the lotus flower; tvam – you; ekaḥ - one; sarvabhūteśaṁ - all living beings; brahmāṇam – of deity Brahmā; upatiṣṭhasi – you attended

***when the boundless self, the person whose residence is the lotus flower, laid down on the lotus, you alone of all the living beings attended to that deity Brahmā.***

## Verse 11

एतत्प्रत्यक्षतः सर्वं पूर्ववृत्तं द्विजोत्तम

तस्मादिच्छामहे श्रोतुं सर्वहेत्वात्मिकां कथाम् (1.11)

**etatpratyakṣataḥ sarvaṁ pūrvavṛttaṁ dvijottama**
**tasmādicchāmahe śrotuṁ sarvahetvātmikāṁ kathām**

etat – this; pratyakṣataḥ - superior perception, insight; sarvaṁ - all; pūrvavṛttaṁ - what occurred before; dvijottama – best of the initiated ritualists; tasmād = tasmāt = therefore; icchāmahe – I wish; śrotuṁ - to hear; sarva – all, everything; hetvātmikāṁ = hetu (cause, origin) + ātmikāṁ (of self ,essential); kathām - how

***You have superior perception of what occurred before, O best of the initiated ritualists, therefore I wish to hear everything about the essential causes.***

## Verse 12

अनुभूतं हि बहुशस्त्वयैकेन द्विजोत्तम

न तेऽस्त्यविदितं किंचित्सर्वलोकेषु नित्यदा (1.12)

**anubhūtaṁ hi bahuśastvayaikena dvijottama**
**na te'styaviditaṁ kiṁcitsarvalokeṣu nityadā**

anubhūtaṁ - knowledgeable; hi – because; bahuśastvayaikena = bahuśas (bahuśah, multiple) + tvaya (by you) + ekena (by one); dvijottama - best of the initiated ritualists; na – no; te – you; 'sty = asti = is; aviditaṁ - not known; kiṁcit - ; sarvalokeṣu – of all the world; nityadā – perpetual

***O best of the initiated ritualists, you alone are knowledgeable about the multiple causes. There is nothing unknown to you about the perpetual situations of these worlds.***

## Verse 13

मार्कण्डेय उवाच

हन्त ते कथयिष्यामि नमस्कृत्वा स्वयम्भुवे

पुरुषाय पुराणाय शाश्वतायाव्ययाय च (1.13)

**mārkaṇḍeya uvāca**
**hanta te kathayiṣyāmi namaskṛtvā svayambhuve**
**puruṣāya purāṇāya śāśvatāyāvyayāya ca**

mārkaṇḍeya - Mārkaṇḍeya; uvāca – said; hanta – O, this is wonderful; te – you; kathayiṣyāmi – I will explain; namaskṛtvā – having offered devoted respect; svayambhuve – in the self-born person; puruṣāya – for the person; purāṇāya – of the ancient one; śāśvatāyāvyayāya = śāśvatāya (eternal, perpetual) + avyayāya (not interrupting, non penetration); ca - and

***Mārkaṇḍeya said:***

***This is wonderful. Offering devoted respects to the self-born person, the ancient personality, who is eternal and who is impenetrable, I will explain everything to you.***

## Verse 14

य एष पृथुदीर्घाक्षः पीतवासा जनार्दनः

एष कर्ता विकर्ता च सर्वभावनभूतकृत् (1.14)

**ya eṣa pṛthudīrghākṣaḥ pītavāsā janārdanaḥ**
**eṣa kartā vikartā ca sarvabhāvanabhūtakṛt**

ya – which; eṣa – this; pṛthudīrghākṣaḥ - one with wide long eyes; pītavāsā – one with yellow garments; janārdanaḥ - Krishna, maintainer of the beings; eṣa – this; kartā – agent, doer; vikartā – transformer; ca – and; sarvabhāvana-bhūtakṛt – one who is the activator of all creatures and existences

***This person with wide long eyes and yellow garments, is Krishna Janārdana, the maintainer of the beings, the agent and transformer, the one who is the activator of all creatures and existences.***

## Verse 15

अचिन्त्यं महदाश्चर्यं पवित्रमपि चोत्तमम्

अनादिनिधनं भूतं विश्वमक्षयमव्ययम् (1.15)

**acintyaṁ mahadāścaryaṁ pavitramapi cottamam**
**anādinidhanaṁ bhūtaṁ viśvamakṣayamavyayam**

acintyaṁ - inconceivable; mahadāścaryaṁ - very surprising, full of wonder; pavitram – pure; api – also; cottamam = ca (and) + uttamam (best); anādinidhanaṁ

- without beginning or ending; bhūtaṁ - substance; viśvam – world; akṣayam – undeteriorating; avyayam – unchanging

***He is inconceivable, full of wonder, pure, the best, without beginning or ending, the substance, the world, undeteriorating and unchanging.***

## Verse 16

एष कर्ता न क्रियते कारणं चापि पौरुषे

यो ह्येनं पुरुषं वेत्ति देवा अपि न तं विदुः (1.16)

**eṣa kartā na kriyate kāraṇaṁ cāpi pauruṣe**
**yo hyenaṁ puruṣaṁ vetti devā api na taṁ viduḥ**

eṣa – this; kartā – producer; na – not; kriyate – performed, produced; kāraṇaṁ - cause; cāpi = ca (and) + api (also); pauruṣe – relating to a personal power; yo = yah = who; hyenaṁ = hy (hi, indeed) + enam (this); puruṣaṁ - person; vetti – know; devā – lower deities; api – also; na – not; taṁ - him; viduḥ - they know

***This person is the producer but he is not produced by anyone. He is the cause of personal power. Indeed, this person knows but the lower deities do not know him.***

## Verse 17

सर्वमाश्चर्यमेवैतन्निर्वृत्तं राजसत्तम

आदितो मनुजव्याघ्र कृत्स्नस्य जगतः क्षये (1.17)

**sarvamāścaryamevaitannirvṛttaṁ rājasattama**
**ādito manujavyāghra kṛtsnasya jagataḥ kṣaye**

sarvamāścaryam – all wonderful; evaitan = eva (also) etan (this); nirvṛttaṁ - without manifestation; rājasattama – best of the kings; ādito = āditah = beginning; manujavyāghra – tiger of men; kṛtsnasya – of the whole; jagataḥ - world; kṣaye - in the destruction

***O best of kings, tiger among men, after the destruction of the world, all of this wonderful creation, which was without manifestation, begins again.***

## Verse 18

चत्वार्याहुः सहस्राणि वर्षाणां तत्कृतं युगम्

तस्य तावच्छती संध्या संध्यांशश्च ततः परम् (1.18)

**catvāryāhuḥ sahasrāṇi varṣāṇāṁ tatkṛtaṁ yugam**
**tasya tāvacchatī saṁdhyā saṁdhyāṁśaśca tataḥ param**

catvāryāhuḥ = catvārya (four) + ahuh (it is said); sahasrāṇi – thousands; varṣāṇāṁ -of years ; tat – that; kṛtaṁ - Era of Easy Achievement; yugam – time cycle, duration; tasya – of this; tāvacchatī – containing hundreds, innumerable; saṁdhyā - dawn; saṁdhyāṁśaś = saṁdhyāṁśah = evening; ca – and; tataḥ - then; param - other

***It is said that four thousand years is the duration of the Era of Easy Achievement. These includes hundreds of dawns and evenings which come one after another.***

## Verse 19

त्रीणि वर्षसहस्राणि त्रेतायुगमिहोच्यते

तस्य तावच्छती संध्या संध्यांशश्च ततः परम् (1.19)

**trīṇi varṣasahasrāṇi tretāyugamihocyate**
**tasya tāvacchatī saṁdhyā saṁdhyāṁśaśca tataḥ param**

trīṇi – three, trifold; varṣa – year; sahasrāṇi – thousands; tretā – Treta Age; yugam – era; ihocyate = iha (here) + ucyate (it is said); tasya – of this; tāvacchatī – containing hundreds; saṁdhyā – dawn, initial stage; saṁdhyāṁśaś = saṁdhyāṁśah = evening, termination stages; ca – and; tataḥ - then, after; param – other

***Three thousand years is said to be the duration of the Treta Era. Of this there are hundreds of initial stages and terminations in sequence.***

## Verse 20

तथा वर्षसहस्रे द्वे द्वापरं परिमाणतः

तस्यापि द्विशती संध्या संध्यांशश्च ततः परम् (1.20)

**tathā varṣasahasre dve dvāparaṁ parimāṇataḥ**
**tasyāpi dviśatī saṁdhyā saṁdhyāṁśaśca tataḥ param**

tathā – as, similarly; varṣa – year; sahasre – in thousands dve; – in two; dvāparaṁ - Dvāpara; parimāṇataḥ - in weight, in duration; tasyāpi = tasya (of this) + api (also); dviśatī – amount of two hundred; saṁdhyā – dawn, initial stage; saṁdhyāṁśaś = saṁdhyāṁśaśh = evening, termination; ca – and; tataḥ - then, after; param – other

***Similarly, there is the Dvāpara Era which is for two thousand years in duration. This has initial stages and terminations occurring in sequence for two hundred years.***

## Verse 21

सहस्रमेकं वर्षाणां ततः कलियुगं स्मृतम्

तस्य वर्षशतं संध्या संध्यांशश्च ततः परम्

संध्यासंध्यांशयोस्तुल्यं प्रमाणमुपधारय (1.21)

**sahasramekaṁ varṣāṇāṁ tataḥ kaliyugaṁ smṛtam**
**tasya varṣaśataṁ saṁdhyā saṁdhyāṁśaśca tata param**
**saṁdhyāsaṁdhyāṁśayostulyaṁ pramāṇamupadhāraya**

sahasramekaṁ - one thousand; varṣāṇāṁ of years; tataḥ - then, next; kaliyugaṁ - Kali Era; smṛtam – it is known; tasya – of this; varṣaśataṁ - hundred year; saṁdhyā dawn, intial stage; saṁdhyāṁśaś = saṁdhyāṁśaḥ = evening, termination; ca – and; tataḥ - after; param – other; saṁdhyā – dawn, initial stage; saṁdhyāṁśayos – of the end or termination; tulyaṁ - same, equal; pramāṇam – duration; upadhāraya – comprehended, understand

***For a duration of one thousand years, the next is the Kali Era. So it is known. This has sequential initial stages and terminations each lasting one hundred years. Understand that the duration of an initial stage and termination are the same.***

## Verse 22

क्षीणे कलियुगे चैव प्रवर्तति कृतं युगम्

एषा द्वादशसाहस्री युगाख्या परिकीर्तिता (1.22)

**kṣīṇe kaliyuge caiva pravartati kṛtaṁ yugam**
**eṣā dvādaśasāhasrī yugākhyā parikīrtitā**

kṣīṇe – in termination; kaliyuge – in Kali era; caiva – and so; pravartati – occurs, commences; kṛtaṁ - Easy Achievement; yugam – Age; eṣā – these; dvādaśa – twelve; sāhasrī – thousand; yugākhyā – eras; parikīrtitā – proclaimed, said

***In the termination of the Kali Era, the Age of Easy Achievement commences again. A cycle of these Eras is twelve thousand years.***

## Verse 23

एतत्सहस्रपर्यन्तमहो ब्राह्ममुदाहृतम्

विश्वं हि ब्रह्मभवने सर्वशः परिवर्तते

लोकानां मनुजव्याघ्र प्रलयं तं विदुर्बुधाः (1.23)

**etatsahasraparyantamaho brāhmamudāhṛtam**
**viśvaṁ hi Brahmā bhavane sarvaśaḥ parivartate**
**lokānāṁ manujavyāghra pralayaṁ taṁ vidurbudhāḥ**

etat – this; sahasra – thousand; paryantam – complete cycle; aho = ahah = day; brāhmam - ; deity Brahmā; udāhṛtam – described, is said; viśvaṁ - the universe; hi – indeed; Brahmā bhavane – existence of deity Brahmā; sarvaśaḥ - all; parivartate – retrogresses; lokānāṁ - of the world; manujavyāghra – tiger among men; pralayaṁ - cosmic dissolution; taṁ - him; vidur = viduh = know, declare; budhāḥ - accomplished yogis

***One thousand complete cycles is said to be a day in the life of the deity Brahmā. Indeed when this universe retrogresses into the existence of deity Brahmā, the accomplished yogis say that the world is in cosmic dissolution, O tiger of men.***

## Verse 24

अल्पावशिष्टे तु तदा युगान्ते भरतर्षभ

सहस्रान्ते नराः सर्वे प्रायशोऽनृतवादिनः (1.24)

**alpāvaśiṣṭe tu tadā yugānte bharatarṣabha**
**sahasrānte narāḥ sarve prāyaśo'nṛtavādinaḥ**

alpāvaśiṣṭe = alpa (small) + avaśiṣṭe (remainder, balance); tu – but; tadā – then; yugānte – at the end of the era; bharatarṣabha – best of the Bharatas; sahasrānte – at the end of one thousand; narāḥ - human beings; sarve – in all; prāyaśo = prāyaśah = generally; 'nṛta = anṛta = without truth, dishonesty; vādinaḥ - speech, speakers

***Then at the end of an era, when a small part of it remains, O best of the Bharatas, at the end of the thousand years, the people in general become untruthful in speech.***

## Verse 25

यज्ञप्रतिनिधिः पार्थ दानप्रतिनिधिस्तथा

व्रतप्रतिनिधिश्चैव तस्मिन्काले प्रवर्तते (1.25)

**yajñapratinidhiḥ pārtha dānapratinidhistathā**
**vratapratinidhiścaiva tasminkāle pravartate**

yajña – religious ceremony; pratinidhiḥ - proxy agent; pārtha – son of Pṛthā; dāna – gifts; pratinidhis = pratinidhih = proxy agent; tathā – as; vrata – commitments; pratinidhiś = pratinidhih = proxy agent; caiva – and so; tasmin – at this; kāle – in time; pravartate – occurs, performs

***At the time, O son of Pṛthā, religious ceremonies are performed by proxy agents, and gifts are given in the same way as well as commitments which are made by substitute agents.***

## Verse 26

ब्राह्मणाः शूद्रकर्माणस्तथा शूद्रा धनार्जकाः

क्षत्रधर्मेण वाप्यत्र वर्तयन्ति गते युगे (1.26)

**brāhmaṇāḥ śūdrakarmāṇastathā śūdrā dhanārjakāḥ**
**kṣatradharmeṇa vāpyatra vartayanti gate yuge**

brāhmaṇāḥ - religious leaders and philosophers; śūdra – laborer; karmāṇas = karmāṇah = social activity; tathā – as; śūdrā – laborers; dhanārjakāḥ - those who focus on acquiring wealth; kṣatradharmeṇa – righteous lifestyle of the government administrators ; vāpyatra = va (or) + api (so) + atra (here); vartayanti – remove, abandon; gate – in the course; yuge – in the era

***Religious leaders and philosophers do the social work of laborers. Laborers act like those who usually focus on acquiring wealth. In the course of the era, those who should have the righteous lifestyle of the government administrators abandon that.***

## Verse 27

निवृत्तयज्ञस्वाध्यायाः पिण्डोदकविवर्जिताः

ब्राह्मणाः सर्वभक्षाश्च भविष्यन्ति कलौ युगे (1.27)

**nivṛttayajñasvādhyāyāḥ piṇḍodakavivarjitāḥ**
**brāhmaṇāḥ sarvabhakṣāśca bhaviṣyanti kalau yuge**

nivṛttaya – of ceasing; jña – knowledge; svādhyāyāḥ - study of the Vedas; piṇḍodaka = piṇḍa (food) + udaka (water); vivarjitāḥ - not offering; brāhmaṇāḥ - priestly and philosophically-inclined persons Brahmā; sarva – all types of food; bhakṣāś - eaters; ca – and; bhaviṣyanti – they become; kalau – in Kali; yuge – in the era

***Ceasing speciality in knowledge and Vedic study, not offering food and water ceremonially to ancestors, the priestly and philosophically-inclined persons become carnivorous in the Kali Era.***

## Verse 28

अजपा ब्राह्मणास्तात शूद्रा जपपरायणाः

विपरीते तदा लोके पूर्वरूपं क्षयस्य तत् (1.28)

**ajapā brāhmaṇāstāta śūdrā japaparāyaṇāḥ**
**viparīte tadā loke pūrvarūpaṁ kṣayasya tat**

ajapā – not reciting sacred sounds; brāhmaṇās- priestly and philosophically-inclined persons; tāta – O dear; śūdrā – laborers; japa - reciting sacred sound; parāyaṇāḥ - those who cherish. are devoted; viparīte - in the opposite; tadā – then; loke – in the world; pūrva – before; rūpaṁ form; kṣayasya – in the destruction of; tat - that

***My dear, the brahmins do not recite sacred sounds, while the laborers become devoted to recitation. Then in the world, everything goes to the contrary, and there is destruction as before.***

## Verse 29

बहवो म्लेच्छराजानः पृथिव्यां मनुजाधिप

मिथ्यानुशासिनः पापा मृषावादपरायणाः (1.29)

**bahavo mleccharājānaḥ pṛthivyāṁ manujādhipa**
**mithyānuśāsinaḥ pāpā mṛṣāvādaparāyaṇāḥ**

bahavo = bahavah = many; mleccha – uncultured class of human beings; rājānaḥ - kings; pṛthivyāṁ - earth; manujādhipa – ruler of human beings; mithyānuśāsinaḥ - mithya (dishonesty) anuśāsinaḥ (addicted to) + pāpā – criminal activities; mṛṣāvāda – false speech, propaganda; parāyaṇāḥ - those who are devoted

***O ruler of human beings, many kings of the uncultured classes will rule over the earth. These persons being devoted to propaganda will condition the people to dishonesty and criminal activities.***

## Verse 30

आन्ध्राः शकाः पुलिन्दाश्च यवनाश्च नराधिपाः

काम्बोजा और्णिकाः शूद्रास्तथाभीरा नरोत्तम (1.30)

**āndhrāḥ śakāḥ pulindāśca yavanāśca narādhipāḥ**
**kāmbojā aurṇikāḥ śūdrāstathābhīrā narottama**

āndhrāḥ - Āndhra tribe; śakāḥ - Śaka tribe; pulindāś = pulindāh = Pulinda tribe; ca – and; yavanāś = yavanāh = Yavana tribe; ca – and; narādhipāḥ - King of human beings; kāmbojā - Kāmbojā tribe; aurṇikāḥ - Aurṇika tribe; śūdrās = śūdrāh = laborers; tathābhīrā = tathā (so) + abhīrā (Abhīra tribe); narottama – best of human beings

***The Āndhra, Śaka, Pulinda, Yavana, Kāmbojā, Aurṇika, and Abhīra tribesmen who are the equivalent of laborers, will prevail O best of the human beings.***

## Verse 31

न तदा ब्राह्मणः कश्चित्स्वधर्ममुपजीवति

क्षत्रिया अपि वैश्याश्च विकर्मस्था नराधिप (1.31)

**na tadā brāhmaṇaḥ kaścitsvadharmamupajīvati**
**kṣatriyā api vaiśyāśca vikarmasthā narādhipa**

na – not; tadā – then; brāhmaṇaḥ - priestly and philosophically-minded persons; kaścit – anyone; svadharmam – personal righteous lifestyle; upajīvati – does; kṣatriyā – administrators and their assistants; api – also; vaiśyāś = vaiśyāh = mercantile people; ca – and; vikarma – deviant activities; sthā – situated, engage in; narādhipa – king of human beings

***Then not one priestly and philosophically-minded person remains committed to the righteous lifestyle for that caste. O king of human beings, the administrators and their assistants and the mercantile people engage in deviant activities.***

## Verse 32

अल्पायुषः स्वल्पबला अल्पतेजःपराक्रमाः

अल्पदेहाल्पसाराश्च तथा सत्याल्पभाषिणः (1.32)

**alpāyuṣaḥ svalpabalā alpatejaḥparākramāḥ**
**alpadehālpasārāśca tathā satyālpabhāṣiṇaḥ**

alpā – short; yuṣaḥ - lifespan svalpabalā = sv (su) (very) + alpa (small) +balā (strength); alpa – little, small; tejaḥ - vitality; parākramāḥ - having much less heroism; alpa – stunted; dehālpa = dehā (bodies) + alpa (dwarf) sārāś = sārāh = power ca – and; tathā – so; satyālpa – reduced truthfulness; bhāṣiṇaḥ - of speech

***People will have short lifespan, very little strength, little vitality and much less heroism. They will have stunted bodies, little power, and be reduced in truthful speech.***

## Verse 33

बहुशून्या जनपदा मृगव्यालावृता दिशः

युगान्ते समनुप्राप्ते वृथा च ब्रह्मचारिणः

भोवादिनस्तथा शूद्रा ब्राह्मणाश्चार्यवादिनः (1.33)

**bahuśūnyā janapadā mṛgavyālāvṛtā diśaḥ**
**yugānte samanuprāpte vṛthā ca Brahmā cāriṇaḥ**
**bhovādinas; tathā śūdrā brāhmaṇāścāryavādinaḥ**

bahuśūnyā – devoid of many people; janapadā – countries; mṛga – wild animal; vyālāvṛtā predatory species; diśaḥ - location, place, the directions, regions; yugānte – at the end of the time cycle; samanuprāpte – taken over by; vṛthā – useless, without value, degraded; ca – and; Brahmā cāriṇaḥ - unmarried student, person who has no carnal knowledge; bho – hey you; vādinas – is called; tathā – as; śūdrā – laborers; brāhmaṇāś = brāhmaṇāh = priestly and philosophically minded persons; cāryavādinaḥ = ca (and) + ārya (honored person, sir) + vādinaḥ (is addressed)

***The countries become devoid of human beings. Predatory species and wild animals spread in all directions. At the end of the era, even persons who have no carnal knowledge are degraded. The laborers call out, 'Hey you!' The priestly and philosophically-minded persons address others saying, 'Yes, Sir.'***

## Verse 34

युगान्ते मनुजव्याघ्र भवन्ति बहुजन्तवः

न तथा घ्राणयुक्ताश्च सर्वगन्धा विशां पते

रसाश्च मनुजव्याघ्र न तथा स्वादुयोगिनः (1.34)

**yugānte manujavyāghra bhavanti bahujantavaḥ**
**na tathā ghrāṇayuktāśca sarvagandhā viś ā ṁ pate**
**rasāśca manujavyāghra na tathā svāduyoginaḥ**

yugānte – at the end of the time cycle; manujavyāghra – tiger of men; bhavanti – they are; bahujantavaḥ - increase in animals; na – no; tathā – so; ghrāṇa – smelling; yuktāś – consumable; ca – and; sarva – all; gandhā – odors; viśāṁ - perfumes, essential oils; pate – o king; rasāś = rasāh = flavors; ca – and; manujavyāghra – tiger-like man; na – not; tathā - and; svādu – sweet; yoginaḥ - union, sensually detected

***At the end of the era, there is an increase in animals. O tiger of men. Also, all odors and essential oils are not as consumable. O king, flavors are not as sweet when sensually detected.***

## Verse 35

बहुप्रजा ह्रस्वदेहाः शीलाचारविवर्जिताः

मुखेभगाः स्त्रियो राजन्भविष्यन्ति युगक्षये (1.35)

**bahuprajā hrasvadehāḥ śīlācāravivarjitāḥ**
**mukhebhagāḥ striyo rājanbhaviṣyanti yugakṣaye**

bahuprajā – many children; hrasva – short, dwarf; dehāḥ - bodies; śīlācāra = śīla (in good character) + ācāra (in behavior); vivarjitāḥ - without devoid of; mukhebhagāḥ - using the mouth as a vagina; striyo = striyah = women; rājan – O king; bhaviṣyanti – they become; yugakṣaye – in the destruction of the era

***There are many children with dwarf bodies, and lacking good character and behavior. O king, the women's mouths function as vaginas when it is the destruction of the era.***

## Verse 36

अट्टशूला जनपदाः शिवशूलाश्चतुष्पथाः

केशशूलाः स्त्रियो राजन्भविष्यन्ति युगक्षये (1.36)

**aṭṭaśūlā janapadāḥ śivaśūlāścatuṣpathāḥ**
**keśaśūlāḥ striyo rājanbhaviṣyanti yugakṣaye**

aṭṭaśūlā – wihout food; janapadāḥ - residences of the citizens; śivaśūlāś - prostitutes; catuṣpathāḥ - highways; keśaśūlāḥ – those without without modesty; striyo = striyah = women; rājan – o king; bhaviṣyanti - will become; yugakṣaye – at the end of the time cycle

***The residences of the citizens will be without food; highways will be littered with prostitutes; women will be immodest, O king, at the end of the time cycle.***

## Verse 37

अल्पक्षीरास्तथा गावो भविष्यन्ति जनाधिप

अल्पपुष्पफलाश्चापि पादपा बहुवायसाः (1.37)

**alpakṣīrāstathā gāvo bhaviṣyanti janādhipa**
**alpapuṣpaphalāścāpi pādapā bahuvāyasāḥ**

alpa – little; kṣīrās - milk; tathā – so; gāvo – cows; bhaviṣyanti – they produce; janādhipa – king of human society; alpa – very little; puṣpa – flower; phalāś = phalāh = fruits; cāpi – and also; pādapā - trees bahu – many; vāyasāḥ - crows

***Cows produce little milk, O king. The trees filled with many crows, produce very little flowers and fruits.***

## Verse 38

ब्रह्मवध्यावलिप्तानां तथा मिथ्याभिशंसिनाम्

नृपाणां पृथिवीपाल प्रतिगृह्णन्ति वै द्विजाः (1.38)

**Brahmā vadhyāvaliptānāṁ tathā mithyābhiśaṁsinām**
**nṛpāṇāṁ pṛthivīpāla pratigṛhṇanti vai dvijāḥ**

Brahmā – priestly and philosophical class of humans; vadhyāva - killing; liptānāṁ - faulted, tainted; tathā – so; sah - he; mithyābhiśaṁsinām – dishonest speech, propaganda; nṛpāṇāṁ - of politicians; pṛthivīpāla – ruler of the earth; pratigṛhṇanti – they appropriate, confiscate; vai – indeed; dvijāḥ - certified ritual priest

***O ruler of the earth, the certified ritual priests, being faulted by their killing of the priestly and philosophical persons, will take favors from politicians who are expert at propaganda.***

## Verse 39

लोभमोहपरीताश्च मिथ्याधर्मध्वजावृताः

भिक्षार्थं पृथिवीपाल चञ्चूर्यन्ते द्विजैर्दिशः (1.39)

**lobhamohaparītāśca mithyādharmadhvajāvṛtāḥ**
**bhikṣārthaṁ pṛthivīpāla cañcūryante dvijairdiśaḥ**

lobha – greed; moha – impractical ideas; parītāś = parītāś = possessed; ca – and; mithyā – false, pretentious; dharma – righteous lifestyle; dhvajā – saintly insignia; vṛtāḥ - showing, exhibting; bhikṣārthaṁ - religious beggars, those worthy of religious donations; pṛthivīpāla – protector of the earth; cañcūryante – they travel here and there; dvijair – by the ritual experts; diśaḥ - the directions

***Being possessed by greed and impractical ideas, exhibiting pretentious religious principles and saintly insignia, the ritual experts travel here and there in various directions. O protector of the earth, they pose as being worthy of religious donations.***

## Verse 40

करभारभयात्पुंसो गृहस्थाः परिमोषकाः

मुनिच्छद्माकृतिच्छन्ना वाणिज्यमुपजीवते (1.40)

**karabhārabhayātpuṁso gṛhasthāḥ parimoṣakāḥ**
**municchadmākṛticchannā vāṇijyamupajīvate**

kara – tax; bhāra – burden, levy; bhayāt – from fear; puṁso = puṁsah = people; gṛhasthāḥ - married couples; parimoṣakāḥ - deceitful people; munic = munih = yogi philosopher; chadmākṛtic = chadma (disguised, pretence) + ākṛtic (dispersed); channā – covered, hidden; vāṇijyam = trade, commerce; upajīvate – is reliant on, dependent on

***Being fearful of taxes, the people, the married couples, become deceitful. The yogi philosopher assumes a disguise and is forced to depend on commerce for a livelihood.***

## Verse 41

मिथ्या च नखरोमाणि धारयन्ति नरास्तदा

अर्थलोभान्नरव्याघ्र वृथा च ब्रह्मचारिणः (1.41)

**mithyā ca nakharomāṇi dhārayanti narāstadā**
**arthalobhānnaravyāghra vṛthā ca Brahmā cāriṇaḥ**

mithyā – false, pretentious; ca – and; nakha – nail; romāṇi – hairs; dhārayanti – they have, assume, are linked to; narās = narās = men; tadā – then; artha – wealth; lobhān – greedy; naravyāghra – tiger-like man; vṛthā - without purpose, worthless; ca – and; Brahmā cāriṇaḥ - celibate yogis

***Then, O tiger among men, the men being pretentious assume nails and hairs of monks. Being greedy for wealth, without purpose, they appear as celibate yogis.***

## Verse 42

आश्रमेषु वृथाचाराः पानपा गुरुतल्पगाः

ऐहलौकिकमीहन्ते मांसशोणितवर्धनम् (1.42)

**āśrameṣu vṛthā cārāḥ pānapā gurutalpagāḥ**
**aihalaukikamīhante māṁsaśoṇitavardhanam**

āśrameṣu - in the home of spiritual teacher, hermitage; vṛthā – worthless, degrading; cārāḥ - behavior, actions; pānapā – alcoholics; guru – those who concern the spiritual teacher; talpagāḥ - those who have sexual intercourse; aiha – desirous; laukikam – popular, vulgar; īhante – they desire; māṁsa – blood; śoṇita – blood; vardhanam – prosperity, abundance

***In the home of the spiritual teacher, they exhibit degrading behaviors. They become alcoholics and are desirous of having sexual intercourse with those who are related to the spiritual teacher. They are desirous of vulgarity and become prosperous by handling flesh and blood.***

## Verse 43

बहुपाषण्डसंकीर्णाः परान्नगुणवादिनः

आश्रमा मनुजव्याघ्र न भवन्ति युगक्षये (1.43)

**bahupāṣaṇḍasaṁkīrṇāḥ parānnaguṇavādinaḥ**
**āśramā manujavyāghra na bhavanti yugakṣaye**

bahu – many, several; pāṣaṇḍa – those who do not believe that there is a God; saṁkīrṇāḥ - scatter-brained; parān - what is contrary; naguṇa – without value, disorderly; vādinaḥ - celebrated speech; āśramā – place of spiritual teacher; manujavyāghra – tiger of men; na - not; bhavanti - they become; yugakṣaye – in the deterioration of the time cycle

***There will be many scatter-brained people who do not believe in God. They will speak highly of what is contrary and disorderly. O tiger-like man, when the time cycle***

***deteriorates, this will be the situation at the home of the spiritual teacher.***

## Verse 44

यथर्तुवर्षी भगवान्न तथा पाकशासनः

न तदा सर्वबीजानि सम्यग्रोहन्ति भारत

अधर्मफलमत्यर्थं तदा भवति चानघ (1.44)

**yathartuvarṣī bhagavānna tathā pākaśāsanaḥ**
**na tadā sarvabījāni samyagrohanti bhārata**
**adharmaphalamatyarthaṁ tadā bhavati cānagha**

yathar – as it should be; tu – but; varṣī – rain; bhagavān – deity Indra; na - not; tathā – so; pākaśāsanaḥ - the subduer of Pāka; na – not; tadā – then; sarva – all; bījāni – seeds; samyag – right, collected; rohanti – they grow, develop; bhārata – O descendant of Bharata; adharma – socially-destructive lifestyle; phalam – fruit, result; atyarthaṁ - exorbitant; tadā – then; bhavati – he becomes; cānagha = ca (and) + ānagha - O gentle entity

***Then the deity Indra, who subdued Pāka, does not give rain as it should be. Most of the seeds planted in the earth do not develop, O descendant of Bharata. A person becomes involved in a socially-destructive lifestyle which yields the corresponding results exorbitantly, O gentle entity.***

## Verse 45

तथा च पृथिवीपाल यो भवेद्धर्मसंयुतः

अल्पायुः स हि मन्तव्यो न हि धर्मोऽस्ति कश्चन (1.45)

**tathā ca pṛthivīpāla yo bhaveddharmasaṁyutaḥ**
**alpāyuḥ sa hi mantavyo na hi dharmo'sti kaścana**

tathā – so; ca – and; pṛthivī – earth; pāla – protector; yo = yaḥ = one who; bhaved = bhavet = become; dharmasaṁyutaḥ - situated in virtuous conduct; alpāyuḥ - short lifespan; sa – he, it; hi – indeed; mantavyo = mantavyah = is regarded; na – not; hi – indeed; dharmo = dharmah = righteous lifestyle; 'sti = asti = is ; kaścana – anyone, whatever, anyway

***O protector of the earth, those who are situated in virtuous conduct, have a short lifespan. Indeed the righteous lifestyle is not regarded by anyone.***

## Verse 46

भूयिष्ठं कूटमानैश्च पण्यं विक्रीणते जनाः

वणिजश्च नरव्याघ्र बहुमाया भवन्त्युत (1.46)

**bhūyiṣṭhaṁ kūṭamānaiśca paṇyaṁ vikrīṇate janāḥ**
**vaṇijaśca naravyāghra bahumāyā bhavantyuta**

bhūyiṣṭhaṁ - most desireous; kūṭamānaiś = kūṭamānaiḥ = by false measure or economic means; ca – and; paṇyaṁ - trade, commodities; vikrīṇate – are sold; janāḥ - people; vaṇijaś = vaṇijaḥ = merchants, businessmen ; ca – and; naravyāghra – tiger-like man; bahumāyā – dishonest means; bhavanty = bhavanti = they operate; uta - moreover

***The people being desirous of commodities are sold with false economic means. Moreover, businessmen, O tiger-like ruler, operate by dishonest methods.***

## Verse 47

धर्मिष्ठाः परिहीयन्ते पापीयान्वर्धते जनः

धर्मस्य बलहानिः स्याद्धर्मश्च बली तथा (1.47)

**dharmiṣṭhāḥ parihīyante pāpīyānvardhate janaḥ**
**dharmasya balahāniḥ syādadharmaśca balī tathā**

dharmiṣṭhāḥ- those who are established in a virtuous lifestyle; parihīyante – become distressed; pāpīyān – criminal elements, dishonest persons; vardhate – thrives; janaḥ - person; dharmasya – of virtue; balahāniḥ - loss of power; syād = syāt = it may be, then there is; adharmaś = adharmaḥ fraudulent means; ca – and; balī – what is authoritive; tathā – as it is

***Those who are established in a virtuous lifestyle become distressed. The person who is dishonest thrives. Then there is the loss of power for virtue and as it is the fraudulent means express authority.***

## Verse 48

अल्पायुषो दरिद्राश्च धर्मिष्ठा मानवास्तदा

दीर्घायुषः समृद्धाश्च विधर्माणो युगक्षये (1.48)

**alpāyuṣo daridrāśca dharmiṣṭhā mānavāstadā**
**dīrghāyuṣaḥ samṛddhāśca vidharmāṇo yugakṣaye**

alpāyuṣo= alpāyuṣaḥ = those with short lifespan; daridrāś = daridrāḥ = those who are poverty-stricken; ca – and; dharmiṣṭhā = dharmiṣṭhāḥ = those who are sincere in the practice of righteous lifestyle; mānavās = mānavāḥ = human beings, people; tadā – then; dīrghāyuṣaḥ - those with long lifespan; samṛddhāś =

samṛddhāḥ = well-situated, with ample income; ca – and; vidharmāṇo = vidharmāṇaḥ = those who are against a righteous lifestyle; yugakṣaye – at the end of the era

***At the end of the era, people who are sincere in the practice of righteous lifestyle become short-lived and poverty-stricken; while those who are against righteous conduct have ample income and become well-situated.***

## Verse 49

अधर्मिष्ठैरुपायैश्च प्रजा व्यवहरन्त्युत

संचयेनापि चाल्पेन भवन्त्याढ्या मदान्विताः (1.49)

**adharmiṣṭhairupāyaiśca prajā vyavaharantyuta**
**saṁcayenāpi cālpena bhavantyāḍhyā madānvitāḥ**

adharmiṣṭhair = adharmiṣṭhaiḥ = by criminal methods; upāyaiś = upāyaiḥ = by a remedy or ruse; ca – and; prajā = prajāḥ = citizens; vyavaharanty = vyavaharanti = they endeavor for; uta – moreover; saṁcayenāpi = saṁcayena (by accumulating) + api (also); cālpena = ca (and) +alpena (by a small); bhavanty = bhavanti = they become; āḍhyā = āḍhyāḥ = those who are wealthy; madānvitāḥ = mada (madness) + anvitāḥ (absorbed in)

***Moreover, the citizens endeavor by ruse and criminal means. By the accumulation of a little money those who are wealthy become mad with pride.***

## Verse 50

धनं विश्वासतो न्यस्तं मिथो भूयिष्ठशो नराः

हर्तुं व्यवसिता राजन्मायाचारसमन्विताः (1.50)

**dhanaṁ viśvāsato nyastaṁ mitho bhūyiṣṭhaśo narāḥ**
**hartuṁ vyavasitā rājanmāyācārasamanvitāḥ**

dhanaṁ - money; viśvāsato = viśvāsataḥ = entrusted in confidence; nyastaṁ - deposited; mitho = mithaḥ = mutual agreement; bhūyiṣṭhaśo = bhūyiṣṭhaśaḥ = eagerly; narāḥ - men; hartuṁ - to confiscate; vyavasitā – which is finished; rājan – O King; māyā – with deceitful methods; cāra – endeavoring; samanvitāḥ - absorbed, completely obsessed by

***Men are eager to confiscate the money entrusted with confidence which was deposited by mutual agreement. Being completely obsessed they figure deceitful methods, declaring that the funds are finished.***

## Verse 51

पुरुषादानि सत्त्वानि पक्षिणोऽथ मृगास्तथा

नगराणां विहारेषु चैत्येष्वपि च शेरते (1.51)

**puruṣādāni sattvāni pakṣiṇo'tha mṛgāstathā**
**nagarāṇāṁ vihāreṣu caityeṣvapi ca śerate**

puruṣādāni – cannibals, predators ; sattvāni – creatures; pakṣiṇo = pakṣiṇaḥ = birds; 'tha = atha = thus; mṛgās = mṛgāḥ = animals; tathā – so; nagarāṇāṁ - of cities; vihāreṣu – in residential places; caityeṣv = caityeṣu =in public assembles ; api – also; ca – and; śerate – lying down

***Cannibals, predators, birds and wild animals lie down in cities, residential places and public assemblies.***

## Verse 52

सप्तवर्षाष्टवर्षाश्च स्त्रियो गर्भधरा नृप

दशद्वादशवर्षाणां पुंसां पुत्रः प्रजायते (1.52)

**saptavarṣāṣṭavarṣāśca striyo garbhadharā nṛpa**
**daśadvādaśavarṣāṇāṁ puṁsāṁ putraḥ prajāyate**

saptavarṣāṣṭavarṣāśca = sapta (seven) + varṣā (years) + aṣṭa (eight) + varṣāś (varṣāḥ- years) + ca (and); striyo = striyaḥ = females, garbhadharā – those who carry a fetus; nṛpa – Oking; daśa – ten; dvādaśa – two and ten; varṣāṇāṁ of years; puṁsāṁ - males; putraḥ - boy; prajāyate – is producing a child

***Females of the age of seven and eight will carry fetuses, O King. Males who are ten and twelve will be the father of children.***

## Verse 53

भवन्ति षोडशे वर्षे नराः पलितिनस्तथा

आयुःक्षयो मनुष्याणां क्षिप्रमेव प्रपद्यते (1.53)

**bhavanti ṣoḍaśe varṣe narāḥ palitinastathā**
**āyuḥkṣayo manuṣyāṇāṁ kṣiprameva prapadyate**

bhavanti – they become; ṣoḍaśe – in sixteen; varṣe – in year; narāḥ - men; palitinas – grey-haired; tathā- just so; āyuḥkṣayo – āyuḥkṣayaḥ the vitality of the body deteriorates; manuṣyāṇāṁ - of people; kṣipram – quickly; eva – indeed; prapadyate – is endured

***Men become grey-haired in their sixteenth year. Indeed the vitality of people's life deteriorates quickly. This must be endured.***

## Verse 54

क्षीणे युगे महाराज तरुणा वृद्धशीलिनः

तरुणानां च यच्छीलं तद्वृद्धेषु प्रजायते (1.54)

**kṣīṇe yuge mahārāja taruṇā vṛddhaśīlinaḥ**
**taruṇānāṁ ca yacchīlaṁ tadvṛddheṣu prajāyate**

kṣīṇe – in the end; yuge – in the era; mahārāja – O great king; taruṇā – youths; vṛddha – elderly person; śīlinaḥ - the temperament; taruṇānāṁ - of youths; ca – and; yac = yat = which; chīlaṁ = śīlaṁ = dispostion, what is becoming of; tad = tat = that; vṛddheṣu – of the elderly persons, regarding those in old age; prajāyate – is displayed

***In the end of the era, O great King, youths will assume the temperament of the elderly, while that which is becoming of the youths will be displayed in the people of old age.***

## Verse 55

विपरीतास्तदा नार्यो वञ्चयित्वा रहः पतीन्

व्युच्चरन्त्यपि दुःशीला दासैः पशुभिरेव च (1.55)

**viparītāstadā nāryo vañcayitvā rahaḥ patīn**
**vyuccarantyapi duḥśīlā dāsaiḥ paśubhireva ca**

viparītās – what is contrary; tadā – then; nāryo = nāryaḥ = women; vañcayitvā – deceiving; rahaḥ - privately, secretly; patīn – husbands; vyuccaranty = vyuccaranti = they deviate sexually; api – also; duḥśīlā

– criminal characters; dāsaiḥ - by servants; paśubhir = paśubhiḥ = by animals; eva – even; ca - and

***Then the women secretly do what is contrary by deceiving their husbands. They deviate sexually with criminal characters, servants and even with animals.***

## Verse 56

तस्मिन्युगसहस्रान्ते संप्राप्ते चायुषः क्षये

अनावृष्टिर्महाराज जायते बहुवार्षिकी (1.56)

**tasminyugasahasrānte saṁprāpte cāyuṣaḥ kṣaye**
**anāvṛṣṭirmahārāja jāyate bahuvārṣikī**

tasmin – in this; yuga – era; sahasrā – thousands; ante – at the end; saṁprāpte – is attained; cāyuṣaḥ = ca (and) + āyuṣaḥ (life time); kṣaye – in the shortening; anāvṛṣṭir = anāvṛṣṭih = drought; mahārāja – o great King; jāyate will continue; bahu – many, several; vārṣikī - years

***In the end of the thousand-year era, when the lifetime is shortened, there will be a drought, O great king, for several years.***

## Verse 57

ततस्तान्यल्पसाराणि सत्त्वानि क्षुधितानि च

प्रलयं यान्ति भूयिष्ठं पृथिव्यां पृथिवीपते (1.57)

**tatastānyalpasārāṇi sattvāni kṣudhitāni ca**
**pralayaṁ yānti bhūyiṣṭhaṁ pṛthivyāṁ pṛthivīpate**

tatas = tataḥ = then; tāny = tāni = they; alpa – little; sārāṇi – strength, vitality; sattvāni – all living beings;

kṣudhitāni – they are very small, diminutive; ca – and; pralayaṁ - end of living beings; yānti – they went; bhūyiṣṭhaṁ - many; pṛthivyāṁ - to earth; pṛthivīpate – Caretaker of the earth

***Then having little vitality, the living beings become small reaching their end. Many of them go into the ground, O caretaker of the earth.***

## Verse 58

ततो दिनकरैर्दीप्तैः सप्तभिर्मनुजाधिप

पीयते सलिलं सर्वं समुद्रेषु सरित्सु च (1.58)

**tato dinakarairdīptaiḥ saptabhirmanujādhipa**
**pīyate salilaṁ sarvaṁ samudreṣu saritsu ca**

tato = tatah = then; dinakarair = dinakaraiḥ = of suns; dīptaiḥ - with beams of light blazing; saptabhir = saptabhiḥ = with seven; manujādhipa – ruler of men; pīyate - is evaporated; salilaṁ - water; sarvaṁ - all; samudreṣu – in the oceans; saritsu – in the rivers; ca - and

***Then O ruler of men, seven blazing suns evaporate all water of oceans and rivers.***

## Verse 59

यच्च काष्ठं तृणं चापि शुष्कं चार्द्रं च भारत

सर्वं तद्भस्मसाद्भूतं दृश्यते भरतर्षभ (1.59)

**yacca kāṣṭhaṁ tṛṇaṁ cāpi śuṣkaṁ cārdraṁ ca bhārata**
**sarvaṁ tadbhasmasādbhūtaṁ dṛśyate bharatarṣabha**

yac = yat = which; ca – and; kāṣṭhaṁ - wood; tṛṇaṁ - grass; cāpi = ca (and) + api (also); śuṣkaṁ - dried; cārdraṁ = ca (and) + ardraṁ (wet); ca – and; bhārata – son of the Bharata family; sarvaṁ - all; tad = tat = that which; bhasmasād = bhasmasāt = from ashes; bhūtaṁ - natural world; dṛśyate = is converted; bharatarṣabha – best of the Bharatas

***O son of the Bharata family, wood and also grass, dried or wet, all of the natural world in fact, will, O best of the Bharatas, be converted into ashes.***

## Verse 60

ततः संवर्तको वह्निर्वायुना सह भारत

लोकमाविशते पूर्वमादित्यैरुपशोषितम् (1.60)

**tataḥ saṁvartako vahnirvāyunā saha bhārata**
**lokamāviśate pūrvamādityairupaśoṣitam**

tataḥ - then; saṁvartako = saṁvartakaḥ = solar flares; vahnir = vahnih = fire; vāyunā - by the wind; saha – with; bhārata – descendant of Bharata; lokam – world; āviśate – is spread; pūrvam – whole, everything; ādityair = ādityaiḥ = by the sun; upaśoṣitam – burnt

***Then O descendant of Bharata, solar flares, fires, along with wind, will spread over everything on the earth which was already parched by the sun.***

## Verse 61

ततः स पृथिवीं भित्त्वा समाविश्य रसातलम्

देवदानवयक्षाणां भयं जनयते महत् (1.61)

**tataḥ sa pṛthivīṁ bhittvā samāviśya rasātalam**
**devadānavayakṣāṇāṁ bhayaṁ janayate mahat**

tataḥ - then; sa – it; pṛthivīṁ - earth; bhittvā – splitting; samāviśya – penetrating; rasātalam – nether region; deva – supernatural controller; dānava – rebellious descedants of Danu; yakṣāṇāṁ - of yaksha nature spirits; bhayaṁ - terror; janayate – is produced; mahat – great

***Then having split the earth, it penetrates to the nether region, producing great terror for the supernatural controllers, the rebellious descendants of Danu and the Yaksha nature spirits.***

## Verse 62

निर्दहन्नागलोकं च यच्च किंचित्क्षिताविह

अधस्तात्पृथिवीपाल सर्वं नाशयते क्षणात् (1.62)

**nirdahannāgalokaṁ ca yacca kiṁcitkṣitāviha**
**adhastātpṛthivīpāla sarvaṁ nāśayate kṣaṇāt**

nirdahan - consuming; nāgalokaṁ - realm of the psychic serpents; ca – and; yac = yat = which; ca – and; kiṁcit – anyone; kṣitāv = kṣitāu = on the ground; iha – here; adhastāt – from below; pṛthivīpāla – protector of the earth; sarvaṁ - all; nāśayate – being annihilated; kṣaṇāt – in a split second

***Consuming the realms of the psychic serpents, and any living creature on the ground, it annihilates in a split second all life, O protector of the earth.***

## Verse 63

ततो योजनविंशानां सहस्राणि शतानि च

निर्दहत्यशिवो वायुः स च संवर्तकोऽनलः (1.63)

**tato yojanaviṁśānāṁ sahasrāṇi śatāni ca**
**nirdahatyaśivo vāyuḥ sa ca saṁvartako'nalaḥ**

tato = tataḥ; yojana – 8 miles; viṁśānāṁ - of twenty; sahasrāṇi – thousands; śatāni – hundreds; ca – and; nirdahaty = nirdahati = it consumes; aśivo = aśivaḥ = inauspicious, unwelcomed; vāyuḥ - wind; sa – it; ca – and; saṁvartako = saṁvartakaḥ = solar flare; 'nalaḥ = analaḥ - fire

***Then the solar flare, that fire, even the unwelcomed wind, consumes hundreds of thousands of 160 miles stretches in distance.***

## Verse 64

सदेवासुरगन्धर्वं सयक्षोरगराक्षसम्

ततो दहति दीप्तः स सर्वमेव जगद्विभुः (1.64)

**sadevāsuragandharvaṁ sayakṣoragarākṣasam**
**tato dahati dīptaḥ sa sarvameva jagadvibhuḥ**

sad = sat – reality; evāsuragandharvaṁ = eva (so) + asura (devilish entities) + gandharvaṁ (celestial musicians); sa – with; yakṣoraga – Yaksha nature spirits and Uraga snakes; rākṣasam – devilish beings; tato = tataḥ = then; dahati – it burns; dīptaḥ - flame; sa – it, sarvam – entire, all; eva – even so; jagad – world; vibhuḥ - spectacular effulgence

***That reality, the flame, the spectacular effulgence burns the entire world consisting of devilish entities, celestial musicians, Yaksha nature spirits, uraga snakes and devilish beings.***

## Verse 65

ततो गजकुलप्रख्यास्तडिन्मालाविभूषिताः

उत्तिष्ठन्ति महामेघा नभस्यद्भुतदर्शनाः (1.65)

**tato gajakulaprakhyāstaḍinmālā vibhūṣitāḥ**
**uttiṣṭhanti mahāmeghā nabhasyadbhutadarśanāḥ**

tato = tataḥ = thereafter; gaja – elephant; kula – herd; prakhyāstaḍin – that which is similar to the rest; mālā – garlands; vibhūṣitāḥ - decorated; uttiṣṭhanti – they rise, float; mahā – great, massive; meghā – clouds; nabhasy = nabhasi = in the sky; adbhutadarśanāḥ - wonderful to see

***Then massive clouds which are similar to herds of elephants and which are wonderful to see, like decorative garlands, float by in the sky.***

## Verse 66

केचिन्नीलोत्पलश्यामाः केचित्कुमुदसंनिभाः

केचित्किञ्जल्कसंकाशाः केचित्पीताः पयोधराः (1.66)

**kecinnīlotpalaśyāmāḥ kecitkumudasaṁnibhāḥ**
**kecitkiñjalkasaṁkāśāḥ kecitpītāḥ payodharāḥ**

kecin = kecit = some; nīlotpala = nīla (blue) + utpala (lily); śyāmāḥ - blueish, blackish; kecit - some; kumuda – night-blooming lotus; saṁnibhāḥ - similar; kecit – some; kiñjal – blossom of lotus; kasaṁ - touchstone;

kāśāḥ - kāśā grass; kecit – some; pītāḥ - yellow; payodharāḥ - milk-laden breasts

***Some (of those clouds) were colored like the blue lily; some were bluish-blackish; some have the hue of the night-blooming lotus; some like touchstone; some like grass; some are yellow and some are like milk-laden breasts.***

## Verse 67

केचिद्धारिद्रसंकाशाः काकाण्डकनिभास्तथा

केचित्कमलपत्राभाः केचिद्धिङ्गुलकप्रभाः (1.67)

**keciddhāridrasaṁkāśāḥ kākāṇḍakanibhāstathā**
**kecitkamalapatrābhāḥ keciddhiṅgulakaprabhāḥ**

kecid = kecit = some; dhāridra = hāridra = turmeric; saṁkāśāḥ - similar to; kāka - crow; āṇḍaka - egg; nibhās – similar to; tathā – as; kecit – some; kamala – lotus; patrā – petals; bhāḥ -brightly colored; kecid = kecit = some; dhiṅgulaka - vermillion; prabhāḥ - effulgence, light

***Some have the color of turmeric. Some are similar to a crow's eggs. Some look like brightly-colored lotus petals. Some have effulgence, being colored like vermillion.***

## Verse 68

केचित्पुरवराकाराः केचिद्गजकुलोपमाः

केचिदञ्जनसंकाशाः केचिन्मकरसंस्थिताः

विद्युन्मालापिनद्धाङ्गाः समुत्तिष्ठन्ति वै घनाः (1.68)

**kecitpuravarākārāḥ kecidgajakulopamāḥ**

**kecidañjanasaṁkāśāḥ kecinmakarasaṁsthitāḥ**
**vidyunmālāpinaddhāṅgāḥ samuttiṣṭhanti vai ghanāḥ**

kecit = some; pura – city; varā – best; kārāḥ - mada, constructed; kecid = kecit = some; gajakulopamāḥ = gajakula (herd of elephants) + upamāḥ - comparative; kecid = kecit = some; añjana – lizard; saṁkāśāḥ - similar to; kecin = kecit = some; makara – crocodile; saṁsthitāḥ - well-situated, remaining poised; vidyun – lightning; mālā – garlands; pinaddhāṅgāḥ - surcharged; samuttiṣṭhanti – they expand; vai – indeed; ghanāḥ - clouds

***Some are like the best constructed cities. Some look like herds of elephants. Some are similar to lizards. Some remain poised like crocodiles. Indeed the clouds expanded and were surcharged with a garland of lightning.***

## Verse 69

घोररूपा महाराज घोरस्वनिनिनादिताः

ततो जलधराः सर्वे व्याप्नुवन्ति नभस्तलम् (1.69)

**ghorarūpā mahārāja ghorasvananināditāḥ**
**tato jaladharāḥ sarve vyāpnuvanti nabhastalam**

ghora – terrible, frightening; rūpā – cloud formations; mahārāja - O King; ghora – rumbling; svananin – noise, sounds; āditāḥ - initially; tato = tataḥ = then; jaladharāḥ - streams of water; sarve - in all directions; vyāpnuvanti – completely pervade; nabhastalam – sky

***O king, initially those terrible cloud formations made rumbling sounds. Then streams of water completely pervaded the sky in all directions.***

## Verse 70

तैरियं पृथिवी सर्वा सपर्वतवनाकरा

आपूर्यते महाराज सलिलौघपरिप्लुता (1.70)

**tairiyaṁ pṛthivī sarvā saparvatavanākarā**
**āpūryate mahārāja salilaughapariplutā**

tair = taiḥ = by those; iyaṁ - this; pṛthivī – on the earth; sarvā – entire; sa – with; parvata – mountain; vanā – forests; karā – mines; āpūryate – is flooded mahārāja – O great King; salilaugha –water; pariplutā – in all directions.

***By those clouds, this entire earth with mountains, forest and mines is flooded with water in all directions, O great King.***

## Verse 71

ततस्ते जलदा घोरा राविणः पुरुषर्षभ

सर्वतः प्लावयन्त्याशु चोदिताः परमेष्ठिना (1.71)

**tataste jaladā ghorā rāviṇaḥ puruṣarṣabha**
**sarvataḥ plāvayantyāśu coditāḥ parameṣṭhinā**

tatas = tataḥ = then; te – those; jaladā – clouds; ghorā – terrible; rāviṇaḥ - drying, roaring; puruṣarṣabha – O best of the human beings; sarvataḥ - everywhere; plāvayanty = plāvayanti = they flood; āśu – quickly; coditāḥ - willed by, destined; parameṣṭhinā – by the Supreme Being Brahmā

***Those terrible clouds roared monstrously, O best of the human beings. As willed by the supreme being, Brahmā, those clouds quickly flooded everywhere.***

## Verse 72

वर्षमाणा महत्तोयं पूरयन्तो वसुंधराम्

सुघोरमशिवं रौद्रं नाशयन्ति च पावकम् (1.72)

**varṣamāṇā mahattoyaṁ pūrayanto vasuṁdharām**
**sughoramaśivaṁ raudraṁ nāśayanti ca pāvakam**

varṣa – rain; māṇā – quantity; mahat – vast; toyaṁ - water; pūrayantoḥ = pūrayantaḥ = pouring; vasuṁdharām – streams of water, downpours; sughoram – very terrible; aśivaṁ - inauspicious; raudraṁ - horrible; nāśayanti – they will extinguish; ca – and; pāvakam – wind and fire

***Pouring a vast quantity of rain with streaming downpours, they extinguish those very terrible, inauspicious and horrible wild fires.***

## Verse 73

ततो द्वादश वर्षाणि पयोदास्त उपप्लवे

धाराभिः पूरयन्तो वै चोद्यमाना महात्मना (1.73)

**tato dvādaśa varṣāṇi payodāsta upaplave**
**dhārābhiḥ pūrayanto vai codyamānā mahātmanā**

tato = tatah = then; dvādaśa – twelve; varṣāṇi – years; payodāsta - water upaplave – in a flood; dhārābhi – raining; pūrayanto = pūrayantaḥ = flood; vai – so it was; codyamānā = ca (and) + udyamānā – invoked; mahātmanā – by the supreme soul

***Then for twelve years water repeatedly rained and flooded; so it was as invoked by the supreme soul.***

## Verse 74

ततः समुद्रः स्वां वेलामतिक्रामति भारत

पर्वताश्च विशीर्यन्ते मही चापि विशीर्यते (1.74)

**tataḥ samudraḥ svāṁ velāmatikrāmati bhārata**
**parvatāśca viśīryante mahī cāpi viśīryate**

tataḥ - then; samudraḥ - ocean; svāṁ - own; velām - limit; atikrāmati – surpass; bhārata – descendant of the Bharatas; parvatāś - parvatāḥ = mountains; ca – and; viśīryante – are broken apart; mahī – planet earth; cāpi – and so; viśīryate – is overwhelmed

***The ocean surpassed its limits, O descendant of the Bharatas. The mountains broke apart. The planet earth was overwhelmed.***

## Verse 75

सर्वतः सहसा भ्रान्तास्ते पयोदा नभस्तलम्

संवेष्टयित्वा नश्यन्ति वायुवेगपराहताः (1.75)

**sarvataḥ sahasā bhrāntāste payodā nabhastalam**
**saṁveṣṭayitvā naśyanti vāyuvegaparāhatāḥ**

sarvataḥ - everywhere; sahasā – suddenly; bhrāntāste – is evaporated; payodā – water; nabhastalam – sky; saṁveṣṭayitvā – having surrounded; naśyanti – are absorbed; vāyu – wind; vega – temptuous; parāhatāḥ - utter devastation

***Then suddenly in all directions, the water was evaporated into the sky. The temptuous winds having surrounded the planet, utterly absorbed everything.***

## Verse 76

ततस्तं मारुतं घोरं स्वयम्भूर्मनुजाधिप

आदिपद्मालयो देवः पीत्वा स्वपिति भारत (1.76)

**tatastaṁ mārutaṁ ghoraṁ svayambhūrmanujādhipa**
**ādipadmālayo devaḥ pītvā svapiti bhārata**

tatas – then; taṁ - it, him; mārutaṁ - storm winds, Maruta; ghoraṁ - terrible; svayambhūr = svayambhūḥ - self-produced deity; manujādhipa – ruler of human society; ādipadmālayo = ādipadmālayaḥ = one whose bed is the lotus; devaḥ - God; pītvā – having swallowed; svapiti – sleep; bhārata – descendant of Bharata

***Then O ruler of human society, descendant of Bharata, having swallowed the terrible storm winds, the self-produced deity, the one whose bed is the lotus, the god, fell asleep.***

## Verse 77

तस्मिन्नेकार्णवे घोरे नष्टे स्थावरजङ्गमे

नष्टे देवासुरगणे यक्षराक्षसवर्जिते (1.77)

**tasminnekārṇave ghore naṣṭe sthāvarajaṅgame**
**naṣṭe devāsuragaṇe yakṣarākṣasavarjite**

tasmin – in this; nekārṇave = na (and) + eka (one) + ārṇave (ocean); ghore ghastly; naṣṭe – are not; sthāvarajaṅgame – mobile and immobile creatures; naṣṭe – are not; devāsuragaṇe beneficent and vindictive supernatural beings; yakṣarākṣasa – nature spirits and devilish beings; varjite – are lacking

***In this situation there is one ghastly ocean. The mobile and immobile creatures cease to exist. The beneficent and vindictive supernatural beings are no more. The nature spirits and devilish beings are lacking.***

## Verse 78

निर्मनुष्ये महीपाल निःश्वापदमहीरुहे

अनन्तरिक्षे लोकेऽस्मिन्भ्रमाम्येकोऽहमादृतः (1.78)

**nirmanuṣye mahīpāla niḥśvāpadamahīruhe**
**anantarikṣe loke'sminbhramāmyeko'hamādṛtaḥ**

nirmanuṣye – without human beings; mahīpāla – ruler of the earth; niḥśvāpada – without wild animals; mahīruhe – what grows in the earth, trees; anantarikṣe – in the sky; loke – on the earth; 'smin = asmin = in this; bhramāmy = bhramāmi = wander; eko = ekaḥ = one person, alone; 'ham = aham = I; ādṛtaḥ - being in a troubled state of mind

***O ruler of the earth, without human beings, without wild animals or trees anywhere in the sky or on the earth, I, being the one person there, wandered about in a troubled state of mind.***

## Verse 79

एकार्णवे जले घोरे विचरन्पार्थिवोत्तम

अपश्यन्सर्वभूतानि वैक्लव्यमगमं परम् (1.79)

**ekārṇave jale ghore vicaranpārthivottama**
**apaśyansarvabhūtāni vaiklavyamagamaṁ param**

ekārṇave – one ocean; jale – in water, ocean; ghore – terrible; vicaran - wandering; pārthivottama – best of the kings of the earth; apaśyan – did not see; sarvabhūtāni – all living beings; vaiklavyam – distress, bewilderment, distress; agamaṁ - came, encounter; param - great

***O best of the kings of the earth, while wandering in that terrible ocean I was distressed and bewildered having not seen or encountered any living beings.***

## Verse 80

ततः सुदीर्घं गत्वा तु प्लवमानो नराधिप

श्रान्तः क्वचिन्न शरणं लभाम्यहमतन्द्रितः (1.80)

**tataḥ sudīrghaṁ gatvā tu plavamāno narādhipa**
**śrāntaḥ kvacinna śaraṇaṁ labhāmyahamatandritaḥ**

tataḥ - then; sudīrghaṁ - very long; gatvā – having gone; tu – but; plavamāno = plavamānaḥ = innundation; narādhipa – O king of men; śrāntaḥ - fatigued; kvacin = kvacit = somewhere; na – not; śaraṇaṁ - shelter; labhāmy = labhāmi = I find; aham – I; atandritaḥ - carefully

***Then wandering about for a long time in the inundation, O king of men, I was fatigued and did not find shelter anywhere.***

## Verse 81

ततः कदाचित्पश्यामि तस्मिन्सलिलसंप्लवे

न्यग्रोधं सुमहान्तं वै विशालं पृथिवीपते (1.81)

**tataḥ kadācitpaśyāmi tasminsalilasaṁplave**
**nyagrodhaṁ sumahāntaṁ vai viśālaṁ pṛthivīpate**

tataḥ - then; kadācit – once; paśyāmi – I see; tasmin – in this; salilasaṁplave – in the waters of that flood; nyagrodhaṁ - banyan fig tree; sumahāntaṁ - enormous; vai – indeed; viśālaṁ - extensive; pṛthivīpate – master of the earth

***Once, I saw in the waters of that flood, an enormous, extensive, banyan fig tree, O master of the earth.***

## Verse 82

शाखायां तस्य वृक्षस्य विस्तीर्णायां नराधिप

पर्यङ्के पृथिवीपाल दिव्यास्तरणसंस्तृते (1.82)

**śākhāyāṁ tasya vṛkṣasya vistīrṇāyāṁ narādhipa**
**paryaṅke pṛthivīpāla divyāstaraṇasaṁstṛte**

śākhāyāṁ - of branches; tasya – of this; vṛkṣasya – of the tree; vistīr = vistīḥ = extensive; ṇāyāṁ - leading part,end; narādhipa – o king of men; paryaṅke – surrounding, covered; pṛthivīpāla – lord of the earth; divyāstaraṇa – divine bedspread; saṁstṛte – completely covered

***O king of men, lord of the earth, attached near the end of the branches of this extensive banyan tree there was a bed which was completely covered with a divine bedspread,***

## Verse 83

उपविष्टं महाराज पूर्णेन्दुसदृशाननम्

फुल्लपद्मविशालाक्षं बालं पश्यामि भारत (1.83)

**upaviṣṭaṁ mahārāja pūrṇendusadṛśānanam**
**phullapadmaviśālākṣaṁ bālaṁ paśyāmi bhārata**

upaviṣṭaṁ - sat, laid upon; mahārāja – O king; pūrṇendusa - full moon; dṛśānanam – of the viewer, appearance; phulla – full blown, dilated; padma – lotus flower; viśālākṣaṁ - extensive, opened; bālaṁ - boy; paśyāmi – I saw; bhārata - descendant of the Bharatas

***O King, there sat someone who appeared like the full moon, whose eyes opened like a full blown lotus. Thus I saw a boy, O descendant of the Bharatas.***

## Verse 84

ततो मे पृथिवीपाल विस्मयः सुमहानभूत्

कथं त्वयं शिशुः शेते लोके नाशमुपागते (1.84)

**tato me pṛthivīpāla vismayaḥ sumahānabhūt**
**kathaṁ tvayaṁ śiśuḥ śete loke nāśamupāgate**

tato = tataḥ = then; me – by me; pṛthivīpāla – king of the earth; vismayaḥ - doubt, astonishment; sumahān – very great; abhūt – felt, existed, manifested; kathaṁ - how; tvayaṁ - by you; śiśuḥ - child; śete loke – of everyone in the world; nāśam - destruction; upāgate – approach, returned

***Then, O king of the earth, a great astonishment was felt by me, regarding how this child could exist here despite the destruction of everyone else in the world.***

## Verse 85

तपसा चिन्तयंश्चापि तं शिशुं नोपलक्षये

भूतं भव्यं भविष्यच्च जानन्नपि नराधिप (1.85)

**tapasā cintayaṁścāpi taṁ śiśuṁ nopalakṣaye**
**bhūtaṁ bhavyaṁ bhaviṣyacca jānannapi narādhipa**

tapasā – by sensually-deprived mystic practice; cintayaṁś = cintayan = contemplated, psyched; cāpi – and so; taṁ - him; śiśuṁ - child; nopalakṣaye = na (not) + upalakṣaye – penetrate; bhūtaṁ - living beings; bhavyaṁ - about to be; bhaviṣyac = bhaviṣyat = in the future; ca – and; jānan – knowing, information; napi = api = also; narādhipa – king of men

***By sensually-deprived mystic practice, I psyched him. I had information of the living beings which are to be, but O king of men, I could not penetrate the nature of that child.***

## Verse 86

अतसीपुष्पवर्णाभः श्रीवत्सकृतलक्षणः

साक्षाल्लक्ष्म्या इवावासः स तदा प्रतिभाति मे (1.86)

**atasīpuṣpavarṇābhaḥ śrīvatsakṛtalakṣaṇaḥ**
**sākṣāllakṣmyā ivāvāsaḥ sa tadā pratibhāti me**

atasī – flax; puṣpa – flower; varṇābhaḥ - having the complexion; śrīvatsa – special golden curl of hair; kṛtalakṣaṇaḥ - possessing the mark; sākṣāl = sākṣāt = directly; lakṣmyā – concerning goddess Lakshmi; ivāvāsaḥ = iva (as if) + āvāsaḥ (residence); sa – he; tadā – then; pratibhāti – appears, seemed to be; me - me

***Having the complexion of the flax flower, possessing the mark of the special golden curl of hair, he seemed to be the residence of the goddess Lakshmi.***

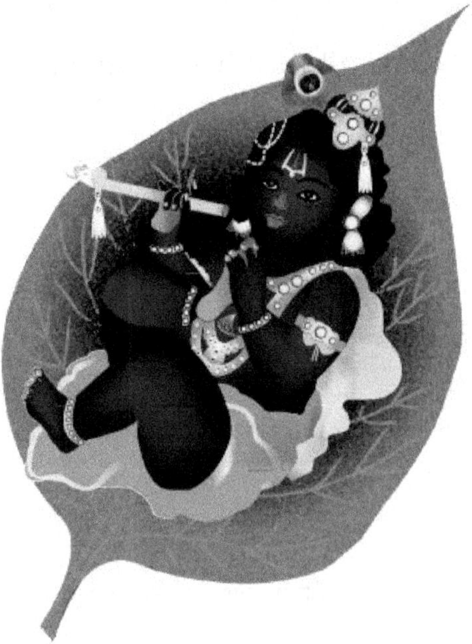

## Verse 87

ततो मामब्रवीद्बालः स पद्मनिभलोचनः

श्रीवत्सधारी द्युतिमान्वाक्यं श्रुतिसुखावहम् (1.87)

**tato māmabravīdbālaḥ sa padmanibhalocanaḥ**
**śrīvatsadhārī dyutimānvākyaṁ śrutisukhāvaham**

tato = tataḥ = then; māma – to me; bravīd = bravīt = addressing ; bālaḥ - child; sa – he; padmanibhalocanaḥ

- one whose eyes are like lotus petals; śrīvatsa – special golden curl of hair; dhārī – one who has; dyutimān – one who is effulgent; vākyaṁ - speech; śruti – words; sukhāvaham – pleasing to hear

***Then addressing me, that child whose eyes were like lotus petals, whose form had the special golden curl of hair, who is effulgent spoke words which were pleasing to hear.***

## Verse 88

जानामि त्वा परिश्रान्तं तात विश्रामकाङ्क्षिणम्

मार्कण्डेय इहास्स्व त्वं यावदिच्छसि भार्गव (1.88)

**jānāmi tvā pariśrāntaṁ tāta viśrāmakāṅkṣiṇam**
**mārkaṇḍeya ihāssva tvaṁ yāvadicchasi bhārgava**

jānāmi – I know; tvā – you; pariśrāntaṁ - thoroughly fatigued; tāta – my dear; viśrāma – take rest; kāṅkṣiṇam – what is dearly wished for; mārkaṇḍeya - Mārkaṇḍeya; ihāssva = iha (here) + āssva (by you); tvaṁ - you; yāvad = yāvat = until, as long as; icchasi - you wish; bhārgava – descendant of Bhrigu

***(The divine child said:)***

***My dear son, I know that you are thoroughly fatigued. You dearly wish to take rest. O Mārkaṇḍeya, descendant of Bhrigu, you may rest here for as long as you wish.***

## Verse 89

अभ्यन्तरं शरीरं मे प्रविश्य मुनिसत्तम

आस्स्व भो विहितो वासः प्रसादस्ते कृतो मया (1.89)

**abhyantaraṁ śarīraṁ me praviśya munisattama**

**āssva bho vihito vāsaḥ prasādaste kṛto mayā**

abhyantaraṁ inside, interior; śarīraṁ - body; me – me; praviśya – entering; munisattama- best of the philosopher-yogis;āssva – you; bho – dear one; vihito = vihitaḥ = ordained; vāsaḥ - residence; prasādaste – I am pleased; kṛto = kṛtaḥ = selected; mayā – by me

***O best of the philosopher-yogis, enter the interior of my body. Live there. O dear one, that is the residence selected by me. I am pleased with you.***

## Verse 90

ततो बालेन तेनैवमुक्तस्यासीत्तदा मम

निर्वेदो जीविते दीर्घे मनुष्यत्वे च भारत (1.90)

**tato bālena tenaivamuktasyāsīttadā mama**
**nirvedo jīvite dīrghe manuṣyatve ca bhārata**

tato = tataḥ = then; bālena – by the boy; tenaiva – as if by him; muktasya – relating to liberation from material existence; āsīt; - was; tadā – then; mama – me; nirvedo = nirvedaḥ = disgust; jīvite – in terms of the life of my body; dīrghe - in long; manuṣya – of being a human being; tve – you; ca – and; bhārata – descendant of Bharata

***Then O descendant of Bharata, by the influence of that boy, there was a feeling of liberation from material existence and a disgust for material existence in terms of the long life of my body and my existence as a human being.***

## Verse 91

ततो बालेन तेनास्यं सहसा विवृतं कृतम्

तस्याहमवशो वक्त्रं दैवयोगात्प्रवेशितः (1.91)

**tato bālena tenāsyaṁ sahasā vivṛtaṁ kṛtam**
**tasyāhamavaśo vaktraṁ daivayogātpraveśitaḥ**

tato = tataḥ = then; bālena – by the boy; tena – by him; āsyaṁ - this sahasā - suddenly; vivṛtaṁ - opened; kṛtam – did; tasya – of this; aham – I; avaśo = avaśaḥ = disempowered; vaktraṁ - mouth; daiva – divine; yogāt – by yoga technique; praveśitaḥ - entered

***Then suddenly that boy opened his mouth. By his divine mystic technique I, who was disempowered, entered him.***

## Verse 92

ततः प्रविष्टस्तत्कुक्षिं सहसा मनुजाधिप

सराष्ट्रनगराकीर्णां कृत्स्नां पश्यामि मेदिनीम् (1.92)

**tataḥ praviṣṭastatkukṣiṁ sahasā manujādhipa**
**sarāṣṭranagarākīrṇāṁ kṛtsnāṁ paśyāmi medinīm**

tataḥ - then; praviṣṭas – entry; tat – that; kukṣiṁ - abdomen; sahasā – suddenly; manujādhipa – king of humanity; sa – with; rāṣṭra - country; nagarā - cities; kīrṇāṁ - scattered, covered; kṛtsnāṁ - entire; paśyāmi – I saw; medinīm - world

***Then O king of humanity, having suddenly entered into his abdomen, I saw the entire world with countries and cities.***

## Verse 93

गङ्गां शतद्रुं सीतां च यमुनामथ कौशिकीम्

चर्मण्वतीं वेत्रवतीं चन्द्रभागां सरस्वतीम् (1.93)

**gaṅgāṁ śatadruṁ sītāṁ ca yamunāmatha kauśikīm**
**carmaṇvatīṁ vetravatīṁ candrabhāgāṁ sarasvatīm**

gaṅgāṁ - Ganges river; śatadruṁ - Shatadru river; sītāṁ - sītā river; ca – and; yamunā - Yamunā river; matha – travelling around; kauśikīm – Kauśikī river; carmaṇvatīṁ - Charmanvati river; vetravatīṁ - Vetravati river; candrabhāgāṁ - Candrabhāgā river; sarasvatīm – Sarasvati river

***While travelling around I saw the Ganges river, the Shatadru, the Sītā, the Yamunā, the Kauśikī, the Charmanvati, the Vetravati, the Candrabhāgā, the Sarasvati,***

## Verse 94

सिन्धुं चैव विपाशां च नदीं गोदावरीमपि

वस्वोकसारां नलिनीं नर्मदां चैव भारत (1.94)

**sindhuṁ caiva vipāśāṁ ca nadīṁ godāvarīmapi**
**vasvokasārāṁ nalinīṁ narmadāṁ caiva bhārata**

sindhuṁ - Sindhu river; caiva – and also; vipāśāṁ - Vipāśā river; ca – and; nadīṁ - rivers; godāvarīm – Godāvarī river; api – also; vasvokasārāṁ - Vasvokasārā river; nalinīṁ - Nalini river; narmadāṁ - Narmada river; caiva – and also; bhārata – descendant of Bharata

***...the Sindhu and also the Vipāśā river, as well as the Godāvarī, the Vasvokasārā, the Nalini and the Narmada, O descendant of Bharata,***

## Verse 95

नदीं ताम्रां च वेण्णां च पुण्यतोयां शुभावहाम्
सुवेणां कृष्णवेणां च इरामां च महानदीम्
शोणं च पुरुषव्याघ्र विशल्यां कम्पुनामपि (1.95)

**nadīṁ tāmrāṁ ca veṇṇāṁ ca puṇyatoyāṁ śubhāvahām**
**suveṇāṁ kṛṣṇaveṇāṁ ca irāmāṁ ca mahānadīm**
**śoṇaṁ ca puruṣavyāghra viśalyāṁ kampunāmapi**

nadīṁ - rivers; tāmrāṁ - Tāmrā river; ca – and; veṇṇāṁ - Veṇṇā river; ca – and; puṇyatoyāṁ - sanctifying waters; śubhāvahām – causing fear; suveṇāṁ - Suvena river; kṛṣṇaveṇāṁ - Krishnavena river; ca – and; irāmāṁ - Irāmā river; ca – and; mahānadīm – Mahānadī river; śoṇaṁ - Śoṇa river; ca – and; puruṣavyāghra – tiger among men; viśalyāṁ - Viśalyā river; kampunām – Kampuna river; api - also

***...rivers Tāmrā and the sanctifying and fear-producing Veṇṇā, the Suvena and Krishnavena, the Irāmā and Mahānadī, the Śoṇa and O tiger among men, the Viśalyā and Kampuna rivers.***

## Verse 96

एताश्चान्याश्च नद्योऽहं पृथिव्यां या नरोत्तम
परिक्रामन्प्रपश्यामि तस्य कुक्षौ महात्मनः (1.96)

**etāścānyāśca nadyo'haṁ pṛthivyāṁ yā narottama**
**parikrāmanprapaśyāmi tasya kukṣau mahātmanaḥ**

etāś = etāḥ = those; cānyāś = ca (and) + anyāḥ (others); ca – and; nadyo = nadyaḥ = rivers; 'haṁ = aham = I; pṛthivyāṁ - earth; yā -which; narottama – best of human beings; parikrāman – touring about; prapaśyāmi – I saw; tasya – of this; kukṣau – in the abdomen; mahātmanaḥ - of the greatest of the souls

***I saw those and other rivers on the earth while touring about, O best of human beings. I saw this in the abdomen of that greatest of the souls.***

## Verse 97

ततः समुद्रं पश्यामि यादोगणनिषेवितम्

रत्नाकरममित्रघ्न निधानं पयसो महत् (1.97)

**tataḥ samudraṁ paśyāmi yādogaṇaniṣevitam**
**ratnākaramamitraghna nidhānaṁ payaso mahat**

tataḥ - then; samudraṁ - ocean; paśyāmi – I saw; yādogaṇa – masses of sea monsters; niṣevitam – inhabited; ratnākaram – jewel mine; amitraghna – killer of enemy forces; nidhānaṁ - refuge, shelter; payaso = payasaḥ = water; mahat - great

***Then O killer of the enemy forces, I saw the ocean, that mine of jewels, the great refuge of water, inhabited by masses of sea monsters.***

## Verse 98

ततः पश्यामि गगनं चन्द्रसूर्यविराजितम्

जाज्वल्यमानं तेजोभिः पावकार्कसमप्रभैः

पश्यामि च महीं राजन्काननैरुपशोभिताम् (1.98)

**tataḥ paśyāmi gaganaṁ candrasūryavirājitam**
**jājvalyamānaṁ tejobhiḥ pāvakārkasamaprabhaiḥ**
**paśyāmi ca mahīṁ rājankānanairupaśobhitām**

tataḥ - there; paśyāmi – I saw; gaganaṁ - sky; candra – moon; sūrya – sun; virājitam – illustrious; jājvalyamānaṁ- blazing; tejobhiḥ - with effulgence; pāvakārka = pāvaka (sun,fire) + arka (relating to the sun); samaprabhaiḥ - with equal splendour; paśyāmi – I saw; ca – and; mahīṁ - vast; rājan – king; = kānanair = kānanaiḥ = with forests; upaśobhitām – very beautiful

***There I saw the sky with the sun and moon, illustrious, blazing with effulgence. The sun was fiery with equal splendor to the sun perceived on the earth before. O king I also saw a vast earth with very beautiful forests.***

## Verse 99

यजन्ते हि तदा राजन्ब्राह्मणा बहुभिः सवैः

क्षत्रियाश्च प्रवर्तन्ते सर्ववर्णानुरञ्जने (1.99)

**yajante hi tadā rājanbrāhmaṇā bahubhiḥ savaiḥ**
**kṣatriyāśca pravartante sarvavarṇānurañjane**

yajante – worship; hi – because; tadā – then; rājan – king; brāhmaṇā – of the priestly and tutorial sector of humanity; bahubhiḥ - with many; savaiḥ - with religious ceremonies; kṣatriyāś = kṣatriyāḥ = government administrators; ca – and; pravartante – they serviced; sarva – all; varṇānurañjane = varṇa (caste) + anurañjane (attachment, love)

***The priestly and tutorial sector of humanity worshiped with many religious ceremonies. The government administrators serviced the other castes with affection.***

## Verse 100

वैश्याः कृषिं यथान्यायं कारयन्ति नराधिप

शुश्रूषायां च निरता द्विजानां वृषलास्तथा (1.100)

**vaiśyāḥ kṛṣiṁ yathānyāyaṁ kārayanti narādhipa**
**śuśrūṣāyāṁ ca niratā dvijānāṁ vṛṣalāstathā**

vaiśyāḥ - mercantile people; kṛṣiṁ - agriculture; yathānyāyaṁ = yathā (as) + anyāyaṁ (others); kārayanti – they craft with skill; narādhipa – king; śuśrūṣāyāṁ - of rendered service; ca – and; niratā – engagement; dvijānāṁ - of the duly trained brahmins; vṛṣalās – laborers; tathā - as

***The mercantile people did agriculture with skill for the benefit of others. O king, the laborers engaged in rendering service to the duly-trained brahmins.***

## Verse 101

ततः परिपतन्राजंस्तस्य कुक्षौ महात्मनः

हिमवन्तं च पश्यामि हेमकूटं च पर्वतम् (1.101)

**tataḥ paripatanrājaṁstasya kukṣau mahātmanaḥ**
**himavantaṁ ca paśyāmi hemakūṭaṁ ca parvatam**

tataḥ - then; paripatan – touring around; rājaṁs = rājan = king; tasya – of this; kukṣau – in the abdomen; mahātmanaḥ - of the supreme soul; himavantaṁ - Himavat; ca – and; paśyāmi – I saw; hemakūṭaṁ - Hemakuta; ca – and; parvatam - mountain

***Thus touring around in the abdomen of that supreme soul, O king, I saw the Himavat and Hemaketu mountains.***

## Verse 102

निषधं चापि पश्यामि श्वेतं च रजताचितम्

पश्यामि च महीपाल पर्वतं गन्धमादनम् (1.102)

**niṣadhaṁ cāpi paśyāmi śvetaṁ ca rajatācitam**
**paśyāmi ca mahīpāla parvataṁ gandhamādanam**

niṣadhaṁ - Niṣadha cāpi – and also; paśyāmi – I saw; śvetaṁ - Śveta; ca – and; rajatācitam – mountain with silver ore; paśyāmi – I saw; ca – and; mahīpāla – king; parvataṁ - mountain; gandhamādanam - Gandhamādana

***I saw the Niṣadha and also the Śveta mountain which has silver ore. I also saw, O king, the Gandhamādana mountain.***

## Verse 103

मन्दरं मनुजव्याघ्र नीलं चापि महागिरिम्

पश्यामि च महाराज मेरुं कनकपर्वतम् (1.103)

**mandaraṁ manujavyāghra nīlaṁ cāpi mahāgirim**
**paśyāmi ca mahārāja meruṁ kanakaparvatam**

mandaraṁ - Mandara; manujavyāghra – tiger among men; nīlaṁ - Nīla cāpi – and also; mahāgirim – huge mountain; paśyāmi – I saw; ca – and; mahārāja – king; meruṁ - Meru; kanaka – gold ore; parvatam - mountain

***O tiger among men, I saw the Mandara and the huge Nīla mountain, as well as the gold mountain, Meru,***

## Verse 104

महेन्द्रं चैव पश्यामि विन्ध्यं च गिरिमुत्तमम्

मलयं चापि पश्यामि पारियात्रं च पर्वतम् (1.104)

**mahendraṁ caiva paśyāmi vindhyaṁ ca girimuttamam**
**malayaṁ cāpi paśyāmi pāriyātraṁ ca parvatam**

mahendraṁ - Mahendra; caiva – and as if; paśyāmi – I saw; vindhyaṁ - Vindhya; ca – and; girim – mountain; uttamam – best; malayaṁ - Malaya; cāpi – and also; paśyāmi - I saw; pāriyātraṁ - Pāriyātra; ca – and; parvatam - mountain

***...the Mahendra and the best of mountains, the Vindhya. I also saw the Malaya and the Pāriyātra mountains.***

## Verse 105

एते चान्ये च बहवो यावन्तः पृथिवीधराः

तस्योदरे मया दृष्टाः सर्वरत्नविभूषिताः (1.105)

**ete cānye ca bahavo yāvantaḥ pṛthivīdharāḥ**
**tasyodare mayā dṛṣṭāḥ sarvaratnavibhūṣitāḥ**

ete – these; cānye = ca (and) +anye (others); ca – and; bahavo = bahavaḥ = many; yāvantaḥ - whatsoever; pṛthivīdharāḥ - protector of the earth; tasyodare – in his abdomen; mayā – by me; dṛṣṭāḥ - were seen; sarva – all; ratna – gems, precious stones; vibhūṣitāḥ - decorated

***These and many others were seen by me in his abdomen, O protector of the earth. All were decorated with gems and precious stones.***

## Verse 106

सिंहान्व्याघ्रान्वराहांश्च नागांश्च मनुजाधिप

पृथिव्यां यानि चान्यानि सत्त्वानि जगतीपते

तानि सर्वाण्यहं तत्र पश्यन्पर्यचरं तदा (1.106)

**siṁhānvyāghrānvarāhāṁśca nāgāṁśca manujādhipa**
**pṛthivyāṁ yāni cānyāni sattvāni jagatīpate**
**tāni sarvāṇyahaṁ tatra paśyanparyacaraṁ tadā**

siṁhān – lions; vyāghrān – tigers; varāhāṁś = varāhān = boars; ca – and; nāgāṁś = nāgān = nāga serpents; ca – and; manujādhipa – ruler of men; pṛthivyāṁ - earth; yāni – they; cānyāni – and others; sattvāni – living beings; jagatīpate – master of the world; tāni – they; sarvāṇy – all; ahaṁ - I; tatra – there; paśyan – saw; paryacaraṁ - travelling around; tadā - then

***Lions, tigers, and boars, nāga serpents, O ruler of men, and other living beings on earth, those I saw while travelling around in that master of the world.***

## Verse 107

कुक्षौ तस्य नरव्याघ्र प्रविष्टः संचरन्दिशः

शक्रादींश्चापि पश्यामि कृत्स्नान्देवगणांस्तथा (1.107)

**kukṣau tasya naravyāghra praviṣṭaḥ saṁcarandiśaḥ**
**śakrādīṁścāpi paśyāmi kṛtsnān devagaṇāṁstathā**

kukṣau – in the abdomen; tasya his; naravyāghra – tiger among men; praviṣṭaḥ - enter; saṁcaran – completely toured; diśaḥ - direction; śakrādīṁś = śakrādīn = Śakra Indra and others; cāpi – and so;

paśyāmi – I saw; kṛtsnān – entire; deva – supernatural rulers; gaṇāṁs = gaṇām = hosts; tathā - as

***O tiger among men, having entered his abdomen, I completely toured in all directions. I also saw Śakra Indra and others, the entire hosts of supernatural beings,***

## Verse 108

गन्धर्वाप्सरसो यक्षानृषींश्चैव महीपते

दैत्यदानवसंघांश्च कालेयांश्च नराधिप

सिंहिकातनयांश्चापि ये चान्ये सुरशत्रवः (1.108)

**gandharvāpsaraso yakṣānṛṣīṁścaiva mahīpate**
**daityadānavasaṁghāṁśca kāleyāṁśca narādhipa**
**siṁhikātanayāṁścāpi ye cānye suraśatravaḥ**

gandharvāpsaraso = gandharvāpsarasaḥ = gandharva (male celestial musicians) + āpsarasaḥ (female angelic beings); yakṣān - Yakṣa nature spirits ṛṣīṁś = ṛṣīn = enlightened yogis; caiva – and so; mahīpate – king; daitya – rebellious sons of Diti; dānava – rebellious sons of Danu; saṁghāṁś = saṁghān = clans; ca – and; kāleyāṁś = kāleyān = Kāleyān = Kāleya clansmen; ca narādhipa – leader of men; siṁhikāta - Siṁhikā's warrior sons; nayāṁś = nayān = leaders; cāpi – and so; ye – they; cānye – and others; sura – assigned supernatural rulers; śatravaḥ - opponents

***...the male celestial musicians, the female angelic beings, the Yaksha nature spirits and the enlightened yogis as well, O King. There were clansmen, the rebellious sons of Diti and Danu, the Kāleyas, the leading set of Simhikā's warrior sons, as well as the assigned supernatural rulers and their other opponents.***

## Verse 109

यच्च किंचिन्मया लोके दृष्टं स्थावरजङ्गमम्

तदपश्यमहं सर्वं तस्य कुक्षौ महात्मनः

फलाहारः प्रविचरन्कृत्स्नं जगदिदं तदा (1.109)

**yacca kiṁcinmayā loke dṛṣṭaṁ sthāvarajaṅgamam**
**tadapaśyamahaṁ sarvaṁ tasya kukṣau mahātmanaḥ**
**phalāhāraḥ pravicarankṛtsnaṁ jagadidaṁ tadā**

yac = yat = this; ca – and; kiṁcin = kiṁcit = everything; mayā – me; loke – in the world; dṛṣṭaṁ - seen; sthāvarajaṅgamam – moving and non-moving living creatures; tada – then; paśyam – saw; ahaṁ - I; sarvaṁ - all; tasya – his; kukṣau –in the abdomen; mahātmanaḥ - supreme soul; phalāhāraḥ - subsisted on fruits; pravicaran – touring about; kṛtsnaṁ - entire, whole; jagad = jagat = world; idaṁ - this; tadā – then, at that time

***Everything in the world was seen by me, all moving and non-moving creatures. I saw it all in the abdomen of that Supreme Soul. At that time subsisting on fruits, I toured the entire world.***

## Verse 110

अन्तः शरीरे तस्याहं वर्षाणामधिकं शतम्

न च पश्यामि तस्याहमन्तं देहस्य कुत्रचित् (1.110)

**antaḥ śarīre tasyāhaṁ varṣāṇāmadhikaṁ śatam**
**na ca paśyāmi tasyāhamantaṁ dehasya kutracit**

antaḥ - inside; śarīre – in the body; tasyāhaṁ = tasya (of this) + ahaṁ (I); varṣāṇām – of years; adhikaṁ - more than; śatam – hundred; na – not; ca – and; paśyāmi – I saw; tasyāham = tasya (his) + aham (I); antaṁ - end; dehasya – of the body; kutracit – anywhere, extent

***Within his body, I existed for hundreds of years. I did not see the end or extent of that body anywhere.***

## Verse 111

सततं धावमानश्च चिन्तयानो विशां पते

आसादयामि नैवान्तं तस्य राजन्महात्मनः (1.111)

**satataṁ dhāvamānaśca cintayāno viśāṁ pate**
**āsādayāmi naivāntaṁ tasya rājanmahātmanaḥ**

satataṁ - always; dhāvamānaś = dhāvamānaḥ = roving about; ca – and; cintayāno - investigating; viśāṁ - penetrating; pate – king; āsādayāmi – I consciously existed; naivāntaṁ = na (not) + eva (so) + antam (end); tasya – his; rājan – king; mahātmana - supreme soul

***Always roving about, investigating and penetrating, O king, I consciously existed but did not find the end to the Supreme Soul.***

## Verse 112

ततस्तमेव शरणं गतोऽस्मि विधिवत्तदा

वरेण्यं वरदं देवं मनसा कर्मणैव च (1.112)

**tatastameva śaraṇaṁ gato'smi vidhivattadā**
**vareṇyaṁ varadaṁ devaṁ manasā karmaṇaiva ca**

tatas = tataḥ = subsequently, then; tam – him; eva – so; śaraṇaṁ - shelter; gato = gatah = went; 'smi = asmi = I; vidhivat – by set procedures or scripture; tadā – then; vareṇyaṁ - one who is distinguished; varadaṁ - one who blesses; devaṁ - God; manasā – by intention; karmaṇa – by action; iva – if; ca - and

***Subsequently, using scriptural procedures, I went to him for shelter. By my actions and intentions I submitted to that distinguished God, the one who bestows blessings.***

## Verse 113

ततोऽहं सहसा राजन्वायुवेगेन निःसृतः

महात्मनो मुखात्तस्य विवृतात्पुरुषोत्तम (1.113)

**tato'haṁ sahasā rājanvāyuvegena niḥsṛtaḥ**
**mahātmano mukhāttasya vivṛtātpuruṣottama**

tato = tataḥ = thereafter; 'haṁ = aham = I; sahasā – suddenly; rājan – king; vāyu – wind; vegena – with gust; niḥsṛtaḥ - released, freed; mahātmano = mahātmanaḥ = supreme soul; mukhāt – from the mouth; tasya – his; vivṛtāt – from opened; puruṣottama – supreme person

***Then O king, being thrust by a gust of wind, I was suddenly released through the opened mouth of the Supreme Soul, the Supreme Person.***

## Verse 114

ततस्तस्यैव शाखायां न्यग्रोधस्य विशां पते

आस्ते मनुजशार्दूल कृत्स्नमादाय वै जगत् (1.114)

**tatastasyaiva śākhāyāṁ nyagrodhasya viśāṁ pate**
**āste manujaśārdūla kṛtsnamādāya vai jagat**

tatas = tatah = then; tasya – his; iva – if; śākhāyāṁ - on a branch; nyagrodhasya of the banyan tree; viśāṁ - lying; pate – king;
āste – sitting; manujaśārdūla – tiger among human beings; kṛtsnam – entire; ādāya – taking together, aggregate; vai – indeed; jagat - world

***Then O king, tiger among human beings, lying on a branch of the banyan tree, there he was as the Aggregate, the whole world.***

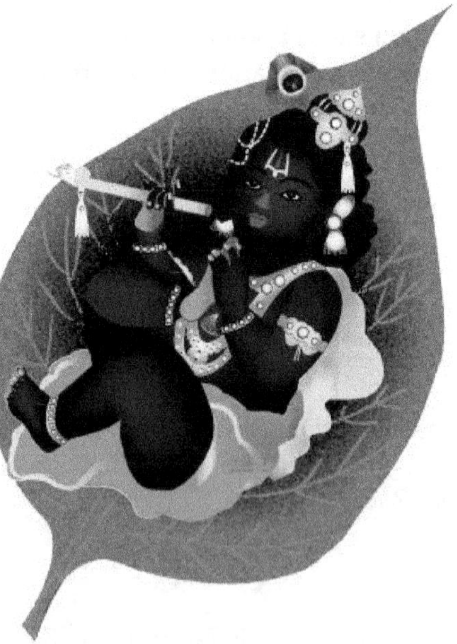

## Verse 115

तेनैव बालवेषेण श्रीवत्सकृतलक्षणम्

आसीनं तं नरव्याघ्र पश्याम्यमिततेजसम् (1.115)

**tenaiva bālaveṣeṇa śrīvatsakṛtalakṣaṇam**
**āsīnaṁ taṁ naravyāghra paśyāmyamitatejasam**

tenaiva = tena (by him) + eva (so); bāla – boy; veṣeṇa – beyond measure, infinite; śrīvatsa – special golden curl of hair; kṛtalakṣaṇam – uniquely marked; āsīnaṁ - seated; taṁ - him; naravyāghra – tiger among men; paśyāmy = paśyāmi = I saw; amita = brilliant; tejasam – of effulgent light

***O tiger among men, I saw him who is beyond measure, the brilliant and effulgent boy who is uniquely marked with the special golden curl of hair.***

## Verse 116

ततो मामब्रवीद्वीर स बालः प्रहसन्निव

श्रीवत्सधारी द्युतिमान्पीतवासा महाद्युतिः (1.116)

**tato māmabravīdvīra sa bālaḥ prahasanniva**
**śrīvatsadhārī dyutimānpītavāsā mahādyutiḥ**

tato = tatah = thereafter; mām – to me; abravīd = abravīt = spoke; vīra – hero; sa – he; bālaḥ - boy; prahasan = laugh; niva = iva = as if; śrīvatsa – special golden curl of hair; dhārī - one who wears; dyutimānpīta – shinning yellow; vāsā – garments; mahādyutiḥ - great effulgence

***Then smiling, the boy, that hero with the special golden curl of hair, the one with shining yellow garments and great effulgence, spoke to me:***

## Verse 117

अपीदानीं शरीरेऽस्मिन्मामके मुनिसत्तम
उषितस्त्वं सुविश्रान्तो मार्कण्डेय ब्रवीहि मे (1.117)

**apīdānīṁ śarīre'sminmāmake munisattama**
**uṣitastvaṁ suviśrānto mārkaṇḍeya bravīhi me**

apīdānīṁ - a timespan; śarīre – in the body; 'smin = asmin = this; māmake – relating to me, mine; munisattama – best of the philosopher yogis; uṣitas – residing, living in; tvaṁ - you; suviśrānto = suviśrāntaḥ = entered deep within; mārkaṇḍeya - Mārkaṇḍeya; bravīhi – I say; me – by me

***O best of the philosopher yogis, Mārkaṇḍeya, for a time you were deep within my body. Listen to what is said by me.***

## Verse 118

मुहूर्तादथ मे दृष्टिः प्रादुर्भूता पुनर्नवा
यया निर्मुक्तमात्मानमपश्यं लब्धचेतसम् (1.118)

**muhūrtādatha me dṛṣṭiḥ prādurbhūtā punarnavā**
**yayā nirmuktamātmānamapaśyaṁ labdhacetasam**

muhūrtād – from the time; atha – thus; me – me; dṛṣṭiḥ - what is perceived; prādurbhūtā – what appeared, insight; punar – again; navā – new; yayā – which; nirmuktam – released from material existence; ātmānam – of the self; apaśyaṁ - saw; labdha – obtained, provided; cetasam – range of consciousness

***Thus from the time that was said to me, a new insight was perceived which provided release from material existence for my spiritual self and a new range of consciousness.***

## Verse 119

तस्य ताम्रतलौ तात चरणौ सुप्रतिष्ठितौ

सुजातौ मृदुरक्ताभिरङ्गुलीभिरलंकृतौ (1.119)

**tasya tāmratalau tāta caraṇau supratiṣṭhitau**
**sujātau mṛduraktābhiraṅgulībhiralaṁkṛtau**

tasya – his; tāmra – copper-colored, red; talau – palms and soles; tāta – dear; caraṇau - two feet; supratiṣṭhitau – well-formed; sujātau – very nice; mṛdu – nice, beautiful; raktābhiraṅgulībhir = raktābhiraṅgulībhiḥ = rakta (red) + ābhiraṅgulībhiḥ (with fingers); alaṁ - yellow; kṛtau – having

***O dear, his copper-colored palms and soles, his very nice well formed feet and beautiful red-colored fingers, have a yellow hue.***

## Verse 120

प्रयतेन मया मूर्ध्ना गृहीत्वा ह्यभिवन्दितौ

दृष्ट्वापरिमितं तस्य प्रभावममितौजसः (1.120)

**prayatena mayā mūrdhnā gṛhītvā hyabhivanditau**
**dṛṣṭvāparimitaṁ tasya prabhāvamamitaujasaḥ**

praya – delight; tena – by him; mayā – me; mūrdhnā – by the head; gṛhītvā - grasping collecting; hy = hi = because; abhivanditau – bowed to the two; dṛṣṭvā – having seen; parimitaṁ - checked all-around; tasya –

his; prabhāvam - influence; amitaujasaḥ - person with infinite effulgent energy

***Having seen his infinite influence and effulgence, with delight, I grasped the two lotus feet while bowing with my head.***

## Verse 121

विनयेनाञ्जलिं कृत्वा प्रयत्नेनोपगम्य च

दृष्टो मया स भूतात्मा देवः कमललोचनः (1.121)

**vinayenāñjaliṁ kṛtvā prayatnenopagamya ca**
**dṛṣṭo mayā sa bhūtātmā devaḥ kamalalocanaḥ**

vinayenāñjaliṁ = vinayena (with submission) + añjaliṁ (joined palms); kṛtvā – having; prayatnenopagamya = prayatnena (with eagernes) + upagamya (approaching); ca – and; dṛṣṭo = dṛṣṭaḥ = saw; mayā – me; sa – he; bhūtātmā – soul of the creatures; devaḥ - God in Person; kamalalocanaḥ - one whose eyes are shaped like lotus petals

***The Soul of all creatures, that God in Person, the one whose eyes are shaped like lotus petals, was seen by me. With joint palms, I approached him eagerly with submission.***

## Verse 122

तमहं प्राञ्जलिर्भूत्वा नमस्कृत्येदमब्रुवम्

ज्ञातुमिच्छामि देव त्वां मायां चेमां तवोत्तमाम् (1.122)

**tamahaṁ prāñjalirbhūtvā namaskṛtyedamabruvam**
**jñātumicchāmi deva tvāṁ māyāṁ cemāṁ tavottamām**

tam – him; ahaṁ - I; prāñjalir = prāñjaliḥ = having joined palms; bhūtvā – having existed; namaskṛtye – offering due worship and attendance; damabruvam – appropriate speech; jñātum – to know; icchāmi – I wish; deva – O God; tvāṁ - you; māyāṁ - mystic creations; cemāṁ - and this; tavottamām – your most spectacular creation

***Having joined palms and offering due worship and attendance with appropriate speech, I said:***

***O God, I wish to know you and also this, your most spectacular creation.***

## Verse 123

आस्येनानुप्रविष्टोऽहं शरीरं भगवंस्तव

दृष्टवानखिलाँल्लोकान्समस्ताञ्जठरे तव (1.123)

**āsyenānupraviṣṭo'haṁ śarīraṁ bhagavaṁstava**
**dṛṣṭavānakhilāṁllokānsamastāñjaṭhare tava**

āsyenānupraviṣṭo = āsyenānupraviṣṭaḥ = āsyena (through the mouth) + ānupraviṣṭaḥ (having entered); 'haṁ = aham = I; śarīraṁ - body; bhagavaṁs = bhagavan = Lord; tava – your; dṛṣṭavān – having seen;akhilāṁl = akhilān = all, entire; lokān – worlds; samastāñ - all; jaṭhare – in the abdomen; tava - your

***Having entered your body through its mouth, O Lord, I saw all the worlds in your abdomen.***

## Verse 124

तव देव शरीरस्था देवदानवराक्षसाः

यक्षगन्धर्वनागाश्च जगत्स्थावरजङ्गमम् (1.124)

**tava deva śarīrasthā devadānavarākṣasāḥ**
**yakṣagandharvanāgāśca jagatsthāvarajaṅgamam**

tava – your; deva – O God; śarīra – body; sthā – existent; deva – assigned supernatural ruler; dānava – powerful devilish sons of Danu; rākṣasāḥ - ordinary mischievous entities; yakṣa - Yaksha nature spirits; gandharva – male celestial musicians; nāgāś = nāgāḥ = Nāga serpents; ca – and; jagat – world; sthāvarajaṅgamam – stationary and mobile creatures

***O God, existent within your body are the assigned supernatural rulers, the powerful devilish sons of Danu, the ordinary mischievous entities, the Yaksha nature spirits and the nāga serpents, in fact all the stationary and mobile creatures in the world.***

## Verse 125

त्वत्प्रसादाच्च मे देव स्मृतिर्न परिहीयते

द्रुतमन्तः शरीरे ते सततं परिधावतः (1.125)

**tvatprasādācca me deva smṛtirna parihīyate**
**drutamantaḥ śarīre te satataṁ paridhāvataḥ**

tvat – by you; prasādāc = prasādāt = due to special favor; ca – and; me – to me; deva – O God; smṛtir = smṛtiḥ = memory; na – not; parihīyate - retained inside; druta – forgotten; mantaḥ - thought; śarīre – in the body; te – your; satataṁ - all; paridhāvataḥ - wandering everywhere

***Due to your special favor to me, O God, the memory of what was inside you as I wandered everywhere through your body, was not forgotten.***

## Verse 126

इच्छामि पुण्डरीकाक्ष ज्ञातुं त्वाहमनिन्दित

इह भूत्वा शिशुः साक्षात्किं भवानवतिष्ठते

पीत्वा जगदिदं विश्वमेतदाख्यातुमर्हसि (1.126)

**icchāmi puṇḍarīkākṣa jñātuṁ tvāhamanindita**
**iha bhūtvā śiśuḥ sākṣātkiṁ bhavānavatiṣṭhate**
**pītvā jagadidaṁ viśvametadākhyātumarhasi**

icchāmi – I wish; puṇḍarīkākṣa - person with lotus eyes; jñātuṁ - to know; tvāham = tva (you) + aham (I); anindita – faultless one; iha – this place; bhūtvā – being; śiśuḥ - child; sākṣāt – directly; kiṁ - why? bhavān – Your Lordship; avatiṣṭhate – establish; pītvā – having swallowed; jagad = jagat = world; idaṁ - this; viśvam – world; etad – this; ākhyātum – to describe; arhasi – you can

***O person with the lotus-shaped eyes, I wish to know you, faultless one. Your Lordship, why as a boy do you stay at this place, having swallowed the world? You may explain this if you can.***

## Verse 127

किमर्थं च जगत्सर्वं शरीरस्थं तवानघ

कियन्तं च त्वया कालमिह स्थेयमरिंदम (1.127)

**kimarthaṁ ca jagatsarvaṁ śarīrasthaṁ tavānagha**
**kiyantaṁ ca tvayā kālamiha stheyamariṁdama**

kim – why; arthaṁ - worth, purpose; ca – and; jagat – world; sarvaṁ - entire; śarīra – body; sthaṁ - existent; tavānagha = tava (your) + anagha (dear one); kiyantaṁ - how much; ca – and; tvayā – by you; kālam – time; iha - this place; stheyam – should stay; ariṁdama – subduer of the rebel souls

***O dear one, for what purpose is the entire world in your body? Time-wise, how much longer will you stay at this place, O subduer of the rebel souls?***

## Verse 128

एतदिच्छामि देवेश श्रोतुं ब्राह्मणकाम्यया

त्वत्तः कमलपत्राक्ष विस्तरेण यथातथम्

महद्ध्येतदचिन्त्यं च यदहं दृष्टवान्प्रभो (1.128)

**etadicchāmi deveśa śrotuṁ brāhmaṇa kāmyayā**
**tvattaḥ kamalapatrākṣa vistareṇa yathātatham**
**mahaddhyetadacintyaṁ ca yadahaṁ dṛṣṭavānprabho**

etad = etat = this; icchāmi – I am eager; deveśa – Lord of the supernatural rulers; śrotuṁ - to hear; brāhmaṇa – for a brahmin; kāmyayā – suitable, desirous; tvattaḥ you; kamalapatrākṣa – one whose eyes are like the lotus petals; vistareṇa – in detail; yathā – as; tatham – precisely; mahad = mahat = enormous, cosmic; dhyetad = dhyetat = link the attention to; acintyaṁ - inconceivable; ca – and; yad = yat = which; ahaṁ - I; dṛṣṭavān – having seen, prabho – honorable one

***I am eager to hear of this, O Lord of the supernatural rulers, for this is suitable information for a brahmin. O lotus-eyed one, explain this in detail, precisely as it develops***

***so that I may be directly linked to this cosmic inconceivable occurrence which I saw in you, O honorable One.***

## Verse 129

इत्युक्तः स मया श्रीमान्देवदेवो महाद्युतिः

सान्त्वयन्मामिदं वाक्यमुवाच वदतां वरः (1.129)

**ityuktaḥ sa mayā śrīmāndevadevo mahādyutiḥ**
**sāntvayanmāmidaṁ vākyamuvāca vadatāṁ varaḥ**

ity = iti = thus; uktaḥ - spoken; sa – he; mayā – me; śrīmān – illustrious person; devadevo = devadeva = God of gods; mahādyutiḥ - greatest effulgence; sāntvayan – endearing person; mām - me; idaṁ - this; vākyam – speaker; uvāca – said; vadatāṁ - lecture; varaḥ - best

***Thus being addressed by me, that illustrious person, the God of gods, the person who is the greatest effulgence, the endearing one, the best of the speakers, gave this lecture.***

# Chapter 12

## Mahabharata:
## Aranyaka (Vana) Parva,
## Markandeya Samasya,
## Chapter 188

## Original / Translation

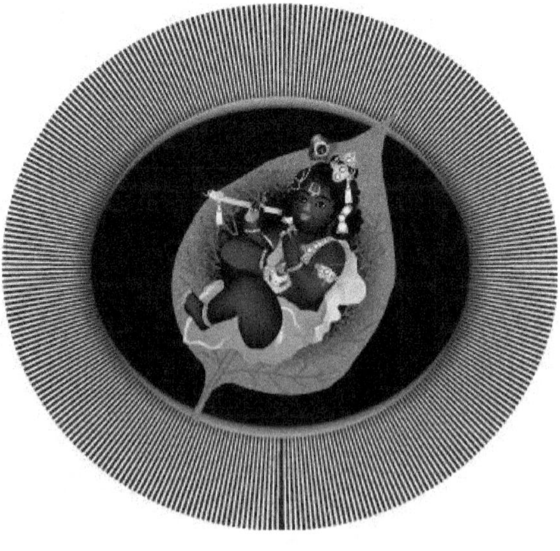

## Verse 1

देव उवाच

कामं देवापि मां विप्र न विजानन्ति तत्त्वतः

त्वत्प्रीत्या तु प्रवक्ष्यामि यथेदं विसृजाम्यहम् (2.1)

**deva uvāca**
**kāmaṁ devāpi māṁ vipra na vijānanti tattvataḥ**
**tvatprītyā tu pravakṣyāmi yathedaṁ visṛjāmyaham**

deva – God, deity; uvāca – said; kāmaṁ - satisfaction; devāpi supernatural rulers even; māṁ - me; vipra – educated mystic priest; na – not; vijānanti – they know; tattvataḥ - detailed truth; tvat – you; prītyā – pleased with; tu – however; pravakṣyāmi – I will explain; yathedaṁ -yatha (so) + idam (this); visṛjāmy = visṛjāmi = I produce; aham - I

***With satisfaction the deity said:***

***Even the supernatural rulers, O educated mystic priest, do not know details of the truth about me. Being pleased with you however, I will explain how I produce this.***

## Verse 2

पितृभक्तोऽसि विप्रर्षे मां चैव शरणं गतः

अतो दृष्टोऽस्मि ते साक्षाद्ब्रह्मचर्यं च ते महत् (2.2)

**pitṛbhakto'si viprarṣe māṁ caiva śaraṇaṁ gataḥ**
**ato dṛṣṭo'smi te sākṣādBrahmā caryaṁ ca te mahat**

pitṛbhakto = pitṛbhaktaḥ = devoted to the ancestors; 'si = asi = you are; vipra – educated mystic priest; rṣe – master teacher of mystic yogis; māṁ - me; caiva – and so; śaraṇaṁ - shelter, reliance; gataḥ - went; ato = ataḥ = therefore; dṛṣṭo = dṛṣṭaḥ = perceived; 'smi = asmi = I am; te – you; sākṣād = sākṣād = directly; Brahmā caryaṁ - yogi whose sexual energy is neutralized; ca – and; te – your; mahat - great

***You are devoted to your ancestors, O educated mystic priest, master teacher of mystic yogis. You came for shelter and directly perceived me. You are a great yogi whose sexual energy is neutralized.***

## Verse 3

आपो नारा इति प्रोक्ताः संज्ञानाम कृतं मया

तेन नारायणोऽस्म्युक्तो मम तद्धयनं सदा (2.3)

**āpo nārā iti proktāḥ saṁjñānāma kṛtaṁ mayā**
**tena nārāyaṇo'smyukto mama taddhyayanaṁ sadā**

āpo = apaḥ = water; nārā - Nārā; iti – thus; proktāḥ - spoken; saṁjñā – known; nāma – name of; kṛtaṁ - was; mayā – me; tena – due to that; nārāyaṇo = nārāyaṇaḥ = God Nārāyaṇa; 'smyukto = asmyuktaḥ = asmy (asmi – I am) + yuktaḥ (identified as); mama – me; tad = tat = that; dhyayanaṁ =dhy (hi - due to) + ayanaṁ (ayana - habitat); sadā - always

***I named the water Nārā. Due to that, I was identified as Nārāyaṇa, since it was always my habitat or ayana.***

## Verse 4

अहं नारायणो नाम प्रभवः शाश्वतोऽव्ययः

विधाता सर्वभूतानां संहर्ता च द्विजोत्तम (2.4)

**ahaṁ nārāyaṇo nāma prabhavaḥ śāśvato'vyayaḥ**
**vidhātā sarvabhūtānāṁ saṁhartā ca dvijottama**

ahaṁ - I; nārāyaṇo = nārāyaṇaḥ = Nārāyaṇa; nāma – titled, called; prabhavaḥ - existential reality; śāśvato = śāśvataḥ = eternal; 'vyayaḥ = avyayaḥ = indestructible; vidhātā – producer; sarvabhūtānāṁ - all living beings; saṁhartā – ultimate destroyer; ca – and; dvijottama – best of the qualified ritualists

***I am the one called Nārāyaṇa, the existential reality, the eternal, the indestructible principle, the producer of all things and ultimate destroyer, O best of the qualified ritualists.***

## Verse 5

अहं विष्णुरहं ब्रह्मा शक्रश्चाहं सुराधिपः

अहं वैश्रवणो राजा यमः प्रेताधिपस्तथा (2.5)

**ahaṁ viṣṇurahaṁ brahmā śakraścāhaṁ surādhipaḥ**
**ahaṁ vaiśravaṇo rājā yamaḥ pretādhipastathā**

ahaṁ - I; viṣṇur = viṣṇuḥ = God Vishnu; ahaṁ - I; brahmā – Procreator Brahmā; śakraś = śakraḥ = Śakra Indra; cāhaṁ = ca (and) + aham (I); surādhipaḥ - Chief Official among the supernatural rulers; ahaṁ - I; vaiśravaṇo = vaiśravaṇaḥ = Vaiśravaṇa Kubera ; rājā – king; yamaḥ - Yama; pretādhipas – deity for the disembodied spirits; tathā - as

***I am the God Vishnu. I am present in Procreator Brahmā, in Śakra Indra, who is the chief official among the supernatural rulers. I am there in King Vaiśravaṇa Kubera, as well as in Yama, the deity for the disembodied spirits.***

## Verse 6

अहं शिवश्च सोमश्च कश्यपश्च प्रजापतिः

अहं धाता विधाता च यज्ञश्चाहं द्विजोत्तम (2.6)

**ahaṁ śivaśca somaśca kaśyapaśca prajāpatiḥ**
**ahaṁ dhātā vidhātā ca yajñaścāhaṁ dvijottama**

ahaṁ - I; śivaś = śivaḥ = Shiva; ca – and; somaś = somaḥ = Soma; ca and; kaśyapaś = kaśyapaḥ = Kaśyapa; ca – and; prajāpatiḥ - primal progenitor; ahaṁ - I; dhātā – Dhātā; vidhātā – Vidhātā; ca – and; yajñaś – effective religious ceremony in person; cāhaṁ = ca (and) + aham (I); dvijottama – o best of the brahmins

***I am present as Shiva, Soma, Kashyapa, and as the primal progenitor. I am there as Dhātā and Vidhātā. I am the effective religious ceremony in person, O best of the brahmins.***

## Verse 7

अग्निरास्यं क्षितिः पादौ चन्द्रादित्यौ च लोचने

सदिशं च नभः कायो वायुर्मनसि मे स्थितः (2.7)

**agnirāsyaṁ kṣitiḥ pādau candrādityau ca locane**
**sadiśaṁ ca nabhaḥ kāyo vāyurmanasi me sthitaḥ**

agnir = agniḥ = fire; āsyaṁ - mouth; kṣitiḥ - earth; pādau – feet; candrādityau = candra (moon) + ādityau (sun); ca – and; locane – eyes; sadiśaṁ - directions; ca – and; nabhaḥ - atmosphere; kāyo = kāyaḥ = body; vāyur = vāyuḥ = wind, air; manasi – as the mind; me – me; sthitaḥ - situated

***The fire is my mouth; the earth, my feet. The sun and moon are my eyes. The atmosphere with the directions is my body. The air is my mind. Thus it is that everything is situated in me.***

## Verse 8

मया क्रतुशतैरिष्टं बहुभिः स्वाप्तदक्षिणैः

यजन्ते वेदविदुषो मां देवयजने स्थितम् (2.8)

**mayā kratuśatairiṣṭaṁ bahubhiḥ svāptadakṣiṇaiḥ**
**yajante vedaviduṣo māṁ devayajane sthitam**

mayā – me; kratu – sacrifices; śatair = śataiḥ = with hundreds; iṣṭaṁ - respectfully completed; bahubhiḥ - with many; svāpta – very skillful; dakṣiṇaiḥ - appropriate gifts; yajante – worship; veda – Veda; viduṣo – expert knowers; māṁ - me; deva – deity; yajane – at the altar; sthitam - situation

***Many hundreds of sacrifices were respectfully and skillfully completed with appropriate gifts by me. The expert knowers of the Vedas worship me as I am situated as the altar of the deity.***

## Verse 9

पृथिव्यां क्षत्रियेन्द्राश्च पार्थिवाः स्वर्गकाङ्क्षिणः

यजन्ते मां तथा वैश्याः स्वर्गलोकजिगीषवः (2.9)

**pṛthivyāṁ kṣatriyendrāśca pārthivāḥ svargakāṅkṣiṇaḥ**
**yajante māṁ tathā vaiśyāḥ svargalokajigīṣavaḥ**

pṛthivyāṁ - earth; kṣatriyendrāś = kṣatriyendrāḥ = rulers who aspire to be Indra; ca – and; pārthivāḥ - rulers of the earth; svarga – heavenly world; kāṅkṣiṇaḥ

- eager to attain; yajante – worship; māṁ - me; tathā – as well as; vaiśyāḥ - business class; svargaloka – celestial places; jigīṣavaḥ - those who are anxious for

***Rulers on earth who aspire to be like Indra, who are eager to attain the heavenly world, worship me, and so do the business class who are anxious to be transferred to the celestial places.***

## Verse 10

चतुःसमुद्रपर्यन्तां मेरुमन्दरभूषणाम्

शेषो भूत्वाहमेवैतां धारयामि वसुंधराम् (2.10)

**catuḥsamudraparyantāṁ merumandarabhūṣaṇām**
**śeṣo bhūtvāhamevaitāṁ dhārayāmi vasuṁdharām**

catuḥ - four; samudra – ocean; paryantāṁ - bounded; meru – Meru; mandara – Mandara; bhūṣaṇām – ornamented, studded; śeṣo = śeṣaḥ = Śeṣa the supernatural serpent; bhūtvāham = bhūtvā (becoming) + aham (I); evaitāṁ = eva (so) +etām (them); dhārayāmi – I support; vasuṁdharām - earth

***Becoming Śeṣa, the supernatural serpent, I support the earth which is bounded by the four seas and studded with the Meru and Mandara mountains.***

## Verse 11

वाराहं रूपमास्थाय मयेयं जगती पुरा

मज्जमाना जले विप्र वीर्येणासीत्समुद्धृता (2.11)

**vārāhaṁ rūpamāsthāya mayeyaṁ jagatī purā**
**majjamānā jale vipra vīryeṇāsītsamuddhṛtā**

vārāhaṁ - Vārāha boar; rūpam – form; āsthāya – assumed; mayeyaṁ = maya (me) + iyam (this); jagatī – world; purā – in the past, long ago; majjamānā - dive; jale – in cosmic water; vipra – educated one; vīryeṇāsīt = vīryeṇa (by courage) + āsīt (was); samuddhṛtā - lifted

***O educated one, long ago, assuming the form of Vārāha the boar, I dove into the cosmic water and courageously lifted this world out of it.***

## Verse 12

अग्निश्च वडवावक्त्रो भूत्वाहं द्विजसत्तम

पिबाम्यपः समाविद्धास्ताश्चैव विसृजाम्यहम् (2.12)

**agniśca vaḍavāvaktro bhūtvāhaṁ dvijasattama**
**pibāmyapaḥ samāviddhāstāścaiva visṛjāmyaham**

agniś = agniḥ = fire; ca – and; vaḍavāvaktro = vaḍavāvaktraḥ = mouth of the horse constellation; bhūtvāhaṁ = bhūtvā (becoming) + ahaṁ (I); dvijasattama – best of the duly-trained brahmins; pibāmy = pibāmi= I drank; apaḥ - water; samāviddhās – agitated; tāś = tāḥ = those; caiva – and so; visṛjāmy = visṛjāmi = create; aham (I)

***Becoming the fire from the mouth of the horse constellation, I, O best of the duly-trained brahmins, drank the water and it is I who agitated and created everything again.***

## Verse 13

ब्रह्म वक्त्रं भुजौ क्षत्रमूरू मे संश्रिता विशः

पादौ शूद्रा भजन्ते मे विक्रमेण क्रमेण च (2.13)

**Brahmā vaktraṁ bhujau kṣatramūrū me saṁśritā viśaḥ**
**pādau śūdrā bhajante me vikrameṇa krameṇa ca**

Brahmā – brahmin; vaktraṁ - mouth; bhujau – arms; kṣatram – political administators; ūrū – thighs; me – mine; saṁśritā – reliance on; viśaḥ - mercantile sector; pādau – feet; śūdrā – laborers; bhajante – were produced; me – mine; vikrameṇa krameṇa – step by step, in sequence; ca - and

***From my mouth, brahmins; from my arms, the political administrators; from my thighs, the mercantile sector of humanity; from my feet, the laborers were produced, in sequence.***

## Verse 14

ऋग्वेदः सामवेदश्च यजुर्वेदोऽप्यथर्वणः

मत्तः प्रादुर्भवन्त्येते मामेव प्रविशन्ति च (2.14)

**ṛgvedaḥ sāmavedaśca yajurvedo'pyatharvaṇaḥ**
**mattaḥ prādurbhavantyete māmeva praviśanti ca**

ṛgvedaḥ - Rig Veda; sāmavedaś = sāmavedaḥ = Sama Veda; ca – and; yajurvedo = yajurvedaḥ = Yajur Veda; 'py = api = as well; atharvaṇaḥ - Atharva Veda; mattaḥ - from me; prādur = prāduḥ = manifest; bhavanty = bhavanti = are; ete – these; mām – me; eva – so; praviśanti - enter; ca - and

***The Rig, Sama, Yajur and Atharva Vedas are manifested from me. These enter into me as well.***

## Verse 15

यतयः शान्तिपरमा यतात्मानो मुमुक्षवः

कामक्रोधद्वेषमुक्ता निःसङ्गा वीतकल्मषाः (2.15)

**yatayaḥ śāntiparamā yatātmāno mumukṣavaḥ**
**kāmakrodhadveṣamuktā niḥsaṅgā vītakalmaṣāḥ**

yatayaḥ - yogis; śānti – spiritual peace; paramā – supreme; yatātmāno = yatātmānaḥ = those disciplined in soul consciousness; mumukṣavaḥ - being eager for liberation; kāma – lust; krodha – anger; dveṣa – envy; muktā – free from; niḥsaṅgā – distant from social associations; vīta – freed from, not having, un (prefix); kalmaṣāḥ - psychologically contaminated

***The yogis, those who have the supreme spiritual peace, those who are disciplined in soul consciousness, those who are eagerly seeking liberation, those who are free from lust, anger and envy, those who are distant from social associations, those who are psychologically uncontaminated,***

## Verse 16

सत्त्वस्था निरहंकारा नित्यमध्यात्मकोविदाः

मामेव सततं विप्राश्चिन्तयन्त उपासते (2.16)

**sattvasthā nirahaṁkārā nityamadhyātmakovidāḥ**
**māmeva satataṁ viprāścintayanta upāsate**

sattvasthā – those who are situated in psychic clarity; nir – without; ahaṁkārā – those without the misplaced sense of identity; nityamadhyātmakovidāḥ - those whose core-selves are centered on the eternal; mām – me; eva – even so; satataṁ - always; viprāś = viprāḥ = educated brahmins; cintayanta – meditative focus; upāsate - worship

***...those who are situated in psychic clarity, those without a misplaced sense of identity, those whose core-selves are centered on the eternal, those educated brahmins worship me with meditative focus.***

## Verse 17

अहं संवर्तको ज्योतिरहं सर्वर्तको यमः

अहं संवर्तकः सूर्यो अहं संवर्तकोऽनिलः (2.17)

**ahaṁ saṁvartako jyotirahaṁ sarvartako yamaḥ**
**ahaṁ saṁvartakaḥ sūryo ahaṁ saṁvartako'nilaḥ**

ahaṁ - I; saṁvartako = saṁvartaka = solar flare; jyotir = jyotiḥ = light; ahaṁ - I; sarvartako = sarvartakaḥ = solar flare; yamaḥ - death personified; ahaṁ - I; saṁvartakaḥ - solar flare; sūryo = sūryaḥ = sun; ahaṁ - I; saṁvartako = saṁvartakaḥ = flare; 'nilaḥ = anilaḥ = air

***I am the solar flare. I am the light of the flare. I am supervisor of death from the solar flare. I am the sun itself, the cosmic flare. I am the air which comprises the solar flare.***

## Verse 18

तारारूपाणि दृश्यन्ते यान्येतानि नभस्तले

मम रूपाण्यथैतानि विद्धि त्वं द्विजसत्तम (2.18)

**tārārūpāṇi dṛśyante yānyetāni nabhastale**

**mama rūpāṇyathaitāni viddhi tvaṁ dvijasattama**

tārā – stars; rūpāṇi – forms; dṛśyante – are perceive; yāny = yāni = they are; etāni – these; nabhastale – in the sky; mama – me; rūpāṇy = rūpāṇi = forms; athaitāni = atha (therefore) + etāni (these); viddhi – know; tvaṁ - you; dvijasattama – best of the duly qualified mystic priests

***Regarding the forms of the stars perceived in the sky, know these as being my forms, O best of the duly-qualified mystic priests.***

## Verse 19

रत्नाकराः समुद्राश्च सर्वं एव चतुर्दिशम्

वसनं शयनं चैव निलयं चैव विद्धि मे (2.19)

**ratnākarāḥ samudrāśca sarva eva caturdiśam**
**vasanaṁ śayanaṁ caiva nilayaṁ caiva viddhi me**

ratnākarāḥ - mines of precious stones; samudrāś = samudrāḥ = oceans; ca – and; sarva – all; eva – also; catur = catuḥ = four; diśam – cardinal points; vasanaṁ - garments; śayanaṁ - resting place; caiva – and also; nilayaṁ - residence; caiva – and also; viddhi – know; me - me

***The mines of precious stones and the oceans, as well as the four cardinal points know these as my garments, resting place and residence.***

## Verse 20

कामं क्रोधं च हर्षं च भयं मोहं तथैव च

ममैव विद्धि रूपाणि सर्वाण्येतानि सत्तम (2.20)

**kāmaṁ krodhaṁ ca harṣaṁ ca bhayaṁ mohaṁ tathaiva ca**
**mamaiva viddhi rūpāṇi sarvāṇyetāni sattama**

kāmaṁ - craving; krodhaṁ - violent disappointment; ca – and; harṣaṁ - pleasure; ca and; bhayaṁ - fear; mohaṁ - delusion; tathaiva – so even; ca – and; mamaiva = mama (me) + eva (too); viddhi – know; rūpāṇi - forms; sarvāṇy = sarvāṇi = all; etāni = these; sattama – best of the reality-perceivers

***Craving, violent disappointment, pleasure, fear and even delusion, know that these too are my forms, O best of the reality-perceivers.***

## Verse 21

प्राप्नुवन्ति नरा विप्र यत्कृत्वा कर्मशोभनम्

सत्यं दानं तपश्चोग्रमहिंसा चैव जन्तुषु (2.21)

**prāpnuvanti narā vipra yatkṛtvā karmaśobhanam**
**satyaṁ dānaṁ tapaścogramahiṁsā caiva jantuṣu**

prāpnuvanti – they achieve; narā – men; vipra – educated brahmin; yat – which; kṛtvā – did; karma – activity; śobhanam – socially-beneficial; satyaṁ - realistic living; dānaṁ - charity; tapaś = tapaḥ - austerity; cogram = ca (and) + ugram (extreme); ahiṁsā – non-violence; caiva – and so; jantuṣu – living beings

***O educated brahmin, whatever people achieve through socially-beneficial activity, realistic living, charity, austerity and extreme non-violence towards all living beings,***

## Verse 22

मद्विधानेन विहिता मम देहविहारिणः

मयाभिभूतविज्ञाना विचेष्टन्ते न कामतः (2.22)

**madvidhānena vihitā mama dehavihāriṇaḥ**
**mayābhibhūtavijñānā viceṣṭante na kāmataḥ**

mad – my; vidhānena – by allowance; vihitā – get; mama – me; deha – body; vihāriṇaḥ - pastime; mayābhibhūta = mayā (me) + abhibhūta (influenced); vijñānā – accommodated, supervision; viceṣṭante – they dance, perform; na – not; kāmataḥ - desire and will power

***...they get by my allowance. Their pastimes are enacted within my body as supervised by me. They perform not by their desire and will but as accommodated by me.***

## Verse 23

सम्यग्वेदमधीयाना यजन्तो विविधैर्मखैः

शान्तात्मानो जितक्रोधाः प्राप्नुवन्ति द्विजातयः (2.23)

**samyagvedamadhīyānā yajanto vividhairmakhaiḥ**
**śāntātmāno jitakrodhāḥ prāpnuvanti dvijātayaḥ**

samyag – thoroughtly; vedam – Veda; adhīyānā – those studying; yajanto = yajantaḥ = doing religious ceremony; vividhair = vividhaih = by various; makhaiḥ - by approved religious ceremony; śāntātmāno = śāntātmānaḥ = spiritually satisfied spiritual self; jitakrodhāḥ - conquering anger; prāpnuvanti – they are rewarded; dvijātayaḥ - those who are duly-qualified ritual priests

***Those who have thoroughly studied the Vedas, those who are spiritually-satisfied, those who conquered anger, those duly-qualified ritual priests are rewarded through the performance of various kinds of approved religious ceremonies.***

## Verse 24

प्राप्तुं न शक्यो यो विद्वन्नरैर्दुष्कृतकर्मभिः

लोभाभिभूतैः कृपणैरनार्यैरकृतात्मभिः (2.24)

**prāptuṁ na śakyo yo vidvannarairduṣkṛtakarmabhiḥ**
**lobhābhibhūtaiḥ kṛpaṇairanāryairakṛtātmabhiḥ**

prāptuṁ- to obtain; na – not; śakyo = śakyaḥ = is possible= ; yo = yaḥ = that which; vidvan – knowing; narair = naraiḥ = by men; duṣkṛt – faulty or criminal acts; akarmabhiḥ - by no benefical social activity; lobhābhibhūtaiḥ - by those who have subdued the impulse for greed; kṛpaṇair = kṛpaṇaiḥ = by the mercy; anāryair = anāryaiḥ = uncultured; akṛt – without; ātmabhiḥ - by the spiritual self

***Know that this is not possible for men who perform faulty or criminal acts, or who render no beneficial social service, or who have not subdued the impulse for greed, or who are without mercy, without culture of the spiritual self.***

## Verse 25

तं मां महाफलं विद्धि पदं सुकृतकर्मणः

दुष्प्रापं विप्रमूढानां मार्गं योगैर्निषेवितम् (2.25)

**taṁ māṁ mahāphalaṁ viddhi padaṁ sukṛtakarmaṇaḥ**
**duṣprāpaṁ vipramūḍhānāṁ mārgaṁ yogairniṣevitam**

taṁ - him; māṁ - me; mahāphalaṁ - great benefits; viddhi – know; padaṁ - foot, position; sukṛta – done nicely; karmaṇaḥ - social activity; duṣprāpaṁ - not acquired; vipra – educatred brahmin; mūḍhānāṁ - of those who are foolish; mārgaṁ - path, method; yogair = yogaiḥ = by yogis; niṣevitam – served, engaged

***Know from me about the great benefits and position of one whose social activities are done nicely. O educated brahmin, that is not acquired by those who are foolish. The yogis engage in the proper method.***

## Verse 26

यदा यदा च धर्मस्य ग्लानिर्भवति सत्तम

अभ्युत्थानमधर्मस्य तदात्मानं सृजाम्यहम् (2.26)

**yadā yadā ca dharmasya glānir bhavati sattama**
**abhyutthānamadharmasya tadātmānaṁ sṛjāmyaham**

yadā yadā = whenever; ca – and; dharmasya – of the righteous lifestyle; glānir = glāniḥ = decrease; bhavati – he becomes; sattama - best of the reality-perceivers; abhyutthānam - increase; adharmasya – of an inappropriate lifestyle, behavior; tad = tat = that; ātmānaṁ - of the self, personally; sṛjāmy = sṛjāmi = appear, make; aham - I

***Whenever there is a decrease of the righteous lifestyle, O best of the reality-perceivers, and an increase in the inappropriate behavior, then I make a personal appearance.***

## Verse 27

दैत्या हिंसानुरक्ताश्च अवध्याः सुरसत्तमैः

राक्षसाश्चापि लोकेऽस्मिन्यदोत्पत्स्यन्ति दारुणाः (2.27)

**daityā hiṁsānuraktāśca avadhyāḥ surasattamaiḥ**
**rākṣasāścāpi loke'sminyadotpatsyanti dāruṇāḥ**

daityā – rebellious sons of Diti; hiṁsānuraktāś = hiṁsā (violence) + anuraktāś (anuraktāḥ - crave); ca – and; avadhyāḥ - not dead, resistance to being killed; surasattamaiḥ - by the best among the supernatural rulers; rākṣasāś = rākṣasāḥ = ordinary mischievious entities; cāpi – as well as; loke – in the world; 'smin – asmin – this; yadotpatsyanti = yadā (when) + utpatsyanti (they roam); dāruṇāḥ - formidable, challenging

***When the rebellious sons of Diti, who crave violence and who are resistant to being killed even by the best of the duly appointed supernatural rulers, as well as the ordinary mischievous entities, roam on this earth, being formidable and challenging,***

## Verse 28

तदाहं संप्रसूयामि गृहेषु शुभकर्मणाम्

प्रविष्टो मानुषं देहं सर्वं प्रशमयाम्यहम् (2.28)

**tadāhaṁ saṁprasūyāmi gṛheṣu śubhakarmaṇām**
**praviṣṭo mānuṣaṁ dehaṁ sarvaṁ praśamayāmyaham**

tad = tat = that; āhaṁ - I; saṁprasūyāmi – I appear; gṛheṣu – in families; śubha – auspicious; karmaṇām – cultural activities; praviṣṭo = praviṣṭaḥ = assuming;

mānuṣaṁ - human; dehaṁ - body; sarvaṁ - all; praśamayāmy = praśamayāmi = I pacify; aham - I

***...I appear in families which are productive of auspicious cultural activities. Assuming a human body, I pacify everyone.***

## Verse 29

सृष्ट्वा देवमनुष्यांश्च गन्धर्वोरगराक्षसान्

स्थावराणि च भूतानि संहराम्यात्ममायया (2.29)

**sṛṣṭvā devamanuṣyāṁśca gandharvoragarākṣasān**
**sthāvarāṇi ca bhūtāni saṁharāmyātmamāyayā**

sṛṣṭvā – having created; deva – supernatural controller; manuṣyāṁś = manuṣyān = human beings; ca – and; gandharvoragarākṣasān = gandharva (celestial musicians) + uraga (serpent) + rākṣasān (mischievous sub-humans); sthāvarāṇi – stationary living creatures; ca – and; bhūtāni – mobile living creatures; saṁharāmy = saṁharāmi = I completely annihilate; ātma – myself; māyayā – by mystic magic

***Having created the supernatural rulers, the human race, the celestial musicians, the uraga serpents, the mischievous sub-humans, I, by mystic magic completely annihilate the stationary and mobile living beings.***

## Verse 30

कर्मकाले पुनर्देहमनुचिन्त्य सृजाम्यहम्

प्रविश्य मानुषं देहं मर्यादाबन्धकारणात् (2.30)

**karmakāle punardehamanucintya sṛjāmyaham**
**praviśya mānuṣaṁ dehaṁ maryādābandhakāraṇāt**

karmakāle – in time of such situation punar = punaḥ - again, repeatedly; deham – body; anucintya – considering; sṛjāmy = sṛjāmi = create; aham – I; praviśya – entering, coming; mānuṣaṁ - human; dehaṁ - body; maryādābandha – keep within the limits, establishing the boundaries; - kāraṇāt – for the reason

***In the time of such situations, I repeatedly consider and create for myself a body, coming as a human being for the purpose of establishing the boundaries of morality.***

## Verse 31

श्वेतः कृतयुगे वर्णः पीतस्त्रेतायुगे मम

रक्तो द्वापरमासाद्य कृष्णः कलियुगे तथा (2.31)

**śvetaḥ kṛtayuge varṇaḥ pītastretāyuge mama**
**rakto dvāparamāsādya kṛṣṇaḥ kaliyuge tathā**

śvetaḥ - white; kṛtayuge – in the Era of Easy Achievement; varṇaḥ - color; pītas – yellow; tretāyuge – in the Tretā Third Era; mama – me; rakto = raktaḥ = red; dvāparam – Era of the devilish deity Dvāpara; āsādya – coming, appearing; kṛṣṇaḥ - blackish; kaliyuge – Era of the Devil Kali; tathā - so

***In the Era of Easy Achievement, I appear with a white complexion. In the Tretā Third Era, I have a yellow color. In the Era of the devilish deity, Dvāpara, I assume a red hue. In the Era of the Devil Kali, I have a blackish tone.***

## Verse 32

त्रयो भागा ह्यधर्मस्य तस्मिन्काले भवन्त्युत

अन्तकाले च संप्राप्ते कालो भूत्वातिदारुणः

त्रैलोक्यं नाशयाम्येकः कृत्स्नं स्थावरजङ्गमम् (2.32)

**trayo bhāgā hyadharmasya tasminkāle bhavantyuta**
**antakāle ca saṁprāpte kālo bhūtvātidāruṇaḥ**
**trailokyaṁ nāśayāmyekaḥ kṛtsnaṁ sthāvarajaṅgamam**

trayo = trayah = three; bhāgā – parts; hy = hi = because; adharmasya – of a socially-destructive lifestyle; tasmin – in this; kāle – in time; bhavanty = bhavanti = become; uta – moreover; antakāle - at the end of time; ca – and; saṁprāpte – is occassioned; kālo = kālaḥ = time; bhūtvātidāruṇaḥ = bhūtvā (becoming) + atidāruṇaḥ (death personified); trailokyaṁ - three sectors of the existential situations; nāśayāmy = nāśayāmi = I destroy; ekaḥ - one; kṛtsnaṁ - whole; sthāvarajaṅgamam – mobile and immobile beings

***Moreover, in time there is a three part (out of four) portion of the socially-destructive lifestyles. At that time, the occasion develops, so I, alone, as death personified, destroy the entire three sectors of this existential situation, which consist of mobile and immobile beings.***

## Verse 33

अहं त्रिवर्त्मा सर्वात्मा सर्वलोकसुखावहः

अभिभूः सर्वगोऽनन्तो हृषीकेश उरुक्रमः (2.33)

**ahaṁ trivartmā sarvātmā sarvalokasukhāvahaḥ**
**abhibhūḥ sarvago'nanto hṛṣīkeśa urukramaḥ**

ahaṁ - I; trivartmā – one who covers everything in three steps; sarvātmā –soul of all beings; sarvaloka – all worlds; sukhāvahaḥ - one who gives happiness; abhibhūḥ - Primary Person in the worlds; sarvago = sarvagaḥ = one who penetrates all simultaneously; 'nanto = anantaḥ = endless; hṛṣīkeśa – Lord of the senses; urukramaḥ - Urukrama who crosses any boundary

***I am the one who covers everything in three steps; the soul of all beings, the person who is all the worlds. I give happiness. I am the Primary Person in these worlds. I penetrate all. I am endless. I am the Lord of the senses. I cross all boundaries.***

## Verse 34

कालचक्रं नयाम्येको ब्रह्मन्नहमरूपि वै

शमनं सर्वभूतानां सर्वलोककृतोद्यमम् (2.34)

**kālacakraṁ nayāmyeko Brahmā nnahamarūpi vai**
**śamanaṁ sarvabhūtānāṁ sarvalokakṛtodyamam**

kālacakraṁ - cycle of time; nayāmy = nayāmi = I will send; eko = ekaḥ - one; Brahmā n – brahmin; naham = aham = I; arūpi – without form; vai – indeed; śamanaṁ - destroyer; sarvabhūtānāṁ - all creatures; sarvaloka – all worlds; kṛtodyamam - motivator

***O brahmin, I, alone, set the cycle of time into motion. I am formless. Indeed, I am the destroyer of all creatures. I am the motivator of all the worlds.***

## Verse 35

एवं प्रणिहितः सम्यङ्मयात्मा मुनिसत्तम

सर्वभूतेषु विप्रेन्द्र न च मां वेत्ति कश्चन (2.35)

**evaṁ praṇihitaḥ samyaṅmayātmā munisattama**
**sarvabhūteṣu viprendra na ca māṁ vetti kaścana**

evaṁ - thus; praṇihitaḥ - ascertained; samyaṅ = samyat = continuing, coherent; mayātmā= mayā (me) + ātmā (spiritual self); munisattama – best of the philosopher-yogis; sarvabhūteṣu – of all beings; viprendra – leader of the educated brahmins; na – not; ca – and; māṁ - me; vetti – know; kaścana - everyone

***Thus ascertained, O best of the philosopher yogis, all beings are penetrated by me but no one knows me, O leader of the educated brahmins.***

## Verse 36

यच्च किंचित्त्वया प्राप्तं मयि क्लेषात्मकं द्विज

सुखोदयाय तत्सर्वं श्रेयसे च तवानघ (2.36)

**yacca kiṁcittvayā prāptaṁ mayi kleṣātmakaṁ dvija**
**sukhodayāya tatsarvaṁ śreyase ca tavānagha**

yac = yat = which; ca – and; kiṁcit – anything; tvayā – by you; prāptaṁ - endured, got; mayi – within me; kleṣātmakaṁ - psychological trauma; dvija – duly trained brahmin; sukhodayāya - increase of happiness; tat – that; sarvaṁ - all; śreyase - in well-being; ca – and; tavānagha = tava (your) + anagha (O faultless one)

***Whatever psychological trauma you endured within my body, O duly-trained brahmin, was for the increase of your happiness and well-being, O faultless one.***

## Verse 37

यच्च किंचित्त्वया लोके दृष्टं स्थावरजङ्गमम्
विहितः सर्वथैवासौ ममात्मा मुनिसत्तम (2.37)

**yacca kiṁcittvayā loke dṛṣṭaṁ sthāvarajaṅgamam**
**vihitaḥ sarvathaivāsau mamātmā munisattama**

yac = yat = which; ca – and; kiṁcit – whatever; tvayā – by you; loke – in the world; dṛṣṭaṁ - seen; sthāvarajaṅgamam – mobile and immobile living creatures; vihitaḥ - established; sarvathaivāsau = sarvatha (in all respects) + eva (so) + asau (he, this); mam – me; ātmā – self; munisattama – best of the philosopher yogis

***Whatever was seen by you in this world of mobile and immobile creatures was in all respects, established by me, who is the self of it all, O best of the philosopher yogis.***

## Verse 38

अर्धं मम शरीरस्य सर्वलोकपितामहः
अहं नारायणो नाम शङ्खचक्रगदाधरः (2.38)

**ardhaṁ mama śarīrasya sarvalokapitāmahaḥ**
**ahaṁ nārāyaṇo nāma śaṅkhacakragadādharaḥ**

ardhaṁ - half; mama – my; śarīrasya – of the body; sarvaloka – all worlds; pitāmahaḥ - great grandfather; ahaṁ - I; nārāyaṇo = nārāyaṇaḥ = God Nārāyaṇa;

nāma – named, known as; śaṅkhacakragadādharaḥ - one who holds the conch, disc and club

***The great grandfather of all these worlds is half of my body. I am known as God Nārāyaṇa, the one who holds the conch, disc and club.***

## Verse 39

यावद्युगानां विप्रर्षे सहस्रपरिवर्तनम्

तावत्स्वपिमि विश्वात्मा सर्वलोकपितामहः (2.39)

**yāvadyugānāṁ viprarṣe sahasraparivartanaṁ**
**tāvatsvapimi viśvātmā sarvalokapitāmahaḥ**

yāvad = yāvat = as; yugānāṁ - of the four eras; viprarṣe – accomplished philosopher-yogi; sahasra – one thousand; parivartanam – transformed into unconsciousness; tāvat – so; svapimi – I sleep; viśvātmā – soul of the universe; sarvalokapitāmahaḥ - great grandfather of all the worlds

***O accomplished philosopher-yogi, for as long as the period of one thousand of the four eras persists, so long I, who am the soul of the universe, the great grandfather of all the worlds, sleep while everyone else is transformed into unconsciousness.***

## Verse 40

एवं सर्वमहं कालमिहासे मुनिसत्तम

अशिशुः शिशुरूपेण यावद्ब्रह्मा न बुध्यते (2.40)

**evaṁ sarvamahaṁ kālamihāse munisattama**
**aśiśuḥ śiśurūpeṇa yāvadbrahmā na budhyate**

evaṁ - thus; sarvam – all; ahaṁ - I; kālam – time; ihāse = iha (here) + ase (exist); munisattama – best of the philosopher yogis; aśiśuḥ - not a child; śiśurūpeṇa by the form of a child; yāvad = yāvat = so long as; brahmā – deity Brahmā; na – not; budhyate – be aware

***Thus O best of the philosopher-yogis, I exist here for all time. Though not a child, I assume the form of a child for as long as the deity Brahmā does not become aware.***

## Verse 41

मया च विप्र दत्तोऽयं वरस्ते ब्रह्मरूपिणा

असकृत्परितुष्टेन विप्रर्षिगणपूजित (2.41)

**mayā ca vipra datto'yaṁ varaste Brahmā rūpiṇā**
**asakṛtparituṣṭena viprarṣigaṇapūjita**

mayā – me; ca – and; vipra – educated brahmin; datto = dattaḥ = given; 'yaṁ = ayam = this; varas – blessing; te – to you; Brahmā rūpiṇā – by the form of exclusive spiritual existence; asakṛt – incessantly, repeatedly; parituṣṭena – by being completely spiritual satisfied; vipra – educated brahmin; rṣi - accomplished philosopher yogi; gaṇa – groups; pūjita - worship

***O educated brahmin, blessings were repeatedly given to you by me who is the form of exclusive spiritual existence. I am completely satisfied by you, O brahmin. You are a person who is worshipped by groups of accomplished philosopher-yogis.***

## Verse 42

सर्वमेकार्णवं दृष्ट्वा नष्टं स्थावरजङ्गमम्

विक्लवोऽसि मया ज्ञातस्ततस्ते दर्शितं जगत् (2.42)

**sarvamekārṇavaṁ dṛṣṭvā naṣṭaṁ sthāvarajaṅgamam**
**viklavo'si mayā jñātastataste darśitaṁ jagat**

sarvam – all; ekārṇavaṁ - one ocean; dṛṣṭvā – having seen; naṣṭaṁ - devastated, wasted; sthāvarajaṅgamam – mobile and immobile creatures; viklavo = viklavaḥ = distressed; 'si – asi = you are; mayā – me; jñātas – known; tat – that; aste – existing; darśitaṁ - shown; jagat - world

***Seeing everything as one vast ocean, with all the mobile and immobile creatures wasted, you were distressed. This was known to me. Thus you were shown that the world still existed (within my body).***

## Verse 43

अभ्यन्तरं शरीरस्य प्रविष्टोऽसि यदा मम

दृष्ट्वा लोकं समस्तं च विस्मितो नावबुध्यसे (2.43)

**abhyantaraṁ śarīrasya praviṣṭo'si yadā mama**
**dṛṣṭvā lokaṁ samastaṁ ca vismito nāvabudhyase**

abhyantaraṁ - inside; śarīrasya – of the body; praviṣṭo = praviṣṭaḥ = entered; 'si = asi = you are; yadā – when; mama – my; dṛṣṭvā – having seen; lokaṁ - world; samastaṁ - everything; ca – and; vismito = vismitaḥ = astonished; nāvabudhyase = na (not) + avabudhyase(you will thoroughly understand)

***Entering the inside of my body, you were astonished. Having seen everything in the world there; you became astonished and did not thoroughly understand.***

## Verse 44

ततोऽसि वक्राद्विप्रर्षे द्रुतं निःसारितो मया

आख्यातस्ते मया चात्मा दुर्ज्ञेयोऽपि सुरासुरैः (2.44)

**tato'si vaktrādviprarṣe drutaṁ niḥsārito mayā**
**ākhyātaste mayā cātmā durjñeyo'pi surāsuraiḥ**

tato = tataḥ = then; 'si = asi = you were; vaktrād = vaktrāt = from the mouth; viprarṣe - accomplished philosopher-yogi; drutaṁ - quickly; niḥsārito = niḥsāritaḥ = expelled; mayā - my; ākhyāt = explained; aste – existing; mayā – my; cātmā = ca (and) + ātmā (special self); durjñeyo = durjñeyaḥ = difficult to ascertain; 'pi = api = also; surāsuraiḥ - by the assigned supernatural rulers and the sorcerers who oppose them

***Then, O accomplished philosopher-yogi, you were quickly expelled through my mouth. I explained about that special self, who is difficult to ascertain even for the assigned supernatural rulers and the sorcerers who oppose them.***

## Verse 45

यावत्स भगवान्ब्रह्मा न बुध्यति महातपाः

तावत्त्वमिह विप्रर्षे विश्रब्धश्चर वै सुखम् (2.45)

**yāvatsa bhagavānbrahmā na budhyati mahātapāḥ**
**tāvattvamiha viprarṣe viśrabdhaścara vai sukham**

yāvat – while; sa – he; bhagavān – lordly deity; brahmā – Procreator Brahmā; na – not; budhyati – he is conscious; mahātapāḥ - one who have greatest mystic austerities to his credit; tāvat – as long as; tvam – you; iha – here; viprarṣe - accomplished philosopher-yogi; viśrabdhaś = viśrabdhaḥ = confidence, trusting; cara – stay; vai – indeed; sukham - hapiness

***While he, the lordly deity, the one with the greatest mystic austerities to his credit, Procreator Brahmā, is not conscious, you can, O accomplished philosopher-yogi, stay here with confidence and happiness.***

## Verse 46

ततो विबुद्धे तस्मिंस्तु सर्वलोकपितामहे

एकीभूतो हि स्त्रक्ष्यामि शरीराद्विजसत्तम (2.46)

**tato vibuddhe tasmiṁstu sarvalokapitāmahe**
**ekībhūto hi srakṣyāmi śarīrāddvijasattama**

tato = tataḥ = then; vibuddhe – in becoming conscious; tasmiṁs = tasmin = in this; tu – but; sarvaloka – all the worlds; pitāmahe – grandsire; ekībhūto = ekībhūtaḥ = one host of living beings, combination; hi – because; srakṣyāmi – I will create; śarīrād = śarīrāt = from the body; dvijasattama – best of the duly trained mystic priests

***Then when that grandsire of all the worlds, becomes conscious, I will create the host of living beings from my body, O best of the duly-trained mystic priests.***

# Verse 47

आकाशं पृथिवीं ज्योतिर्वायुं सलिलमेव च

लोके यच्च भवेच्छेषमिह स्थावरजङ्गमम् (2.47)

**ākāśaṁ pṛthivīṁ jyotirvāyuṁ salilameva ca**
**loke yacca bhavecchеṣamiha sthāvarajaṅgamam**

ākāśaṁ - sky; pṛthivīṁ - earth; jyotir = jyotiḥ = light; vāyuṁ - wind; salilam – water; eva – so; ca – and; loke – in the world; yac = yat = which; ca – and; bhavec = bhavet = become; cheṣam = śeṣam = what remains, everything not mentioned; iha – here; sthāvarajaṅgamam – mobile and immobile creatures

***There will be the sky, the earth, the light, the wind, the water even and everything else for this world, all the mobile and immobile creatures.***

# Verse 48

मार्कण्डेय उवाच

इत्युक्त्वान्तर्हितस्तात स देवः परमाद्भुतः

प्रजाश्चेमाः प्रपश्यामि विचित्रा बहुधाकृताः (2.48)

**mārkaṇḍeya uvāca**
**ityuktvāntarhitastāta sa devaḥ paramādbhutaḥ**
**prajāścemāḥ prapaśyāmi vicitrā bahudhākṛtāḥ**

mārkaṇḍeya - Mārkaṇḍeya; uvāca – said; ity = iti = thus; uktvā – having said; antarhitas = antaḥhitas = invisible; tāta – dear one; sa – he; devaḥ - God; param - greatest; ādbhutaḥ - wonderful being; prajāś = prajāḥ = living beings; cemāḥ = ca (and) + imāḥ (these);

prapaśyāmi – I saw; vicitrā – variegated; bahudhā – infinitely dispersed; kṛtāḥ - existed

***Mārkaṇḍeya said:***

***O dear one, having said that, the God, the greatest, most spectacular living being, became invisible. I saw these beings, this variegated infinitely-dispersed creation, existing again.***

## Verse 49

एतद्दृष्टं मया राजंस्तस्मिन्प्राप्ते युगक्षये

आश्चर्यं भरतश्रेष्ठ सर्वधर्मभृतां वर (2.49)

**etaddṛṣṭaṁ mayā rājaṁstasminprāpte yugakṣaye**
**āścaryaṁ bharataśreṣṭha sarvadharmabhṛtāṁ vara**

etad = etat = this; dṛṣṭaṁ - saw; mayā – my; rājaṁs = rājan = king; tasmin – in this; prāpte – acquired, experienced; yugakṣaye – at the end of the era; āścaryaṁ - wonder; bharataśreṣṭha – best of the Bharatas; sarva – all; dharma = virtuous lifestyle; bhṛtāṁ - supported; vara- best

***This was seen by me O king. At the end of the era, I experienced that wonder, O best of the Bharatas, best of all those who support the virtuous lifestyle.***

## Verse 50

यः स देवो मया दृष्टः पुरा पद्मनिभेक्षणः

स एष पुरुषव्याघ्र संबन्धी ते जनार्दनः (2.50)

**yaḥ sa devo mayā dṛṣṭaḥ purā padmanibhekṣaṇaḥ**
**sa eṣa puruṣavyāghra saṁbandhī te janārdanaḥ**

yaḥ - who; sa – he; devo = devaḥ = God; mayā – me; dṛṣṭaḥ - seen; purā – long long ago; padmanibhekṣaṇaḥ - person with eyes like lotus petals; sa – he; eṣa – this; puruṣavyāghra – tiger among men; saṁbandhī - in connection, family members; te – your; janārdanaḥ - Janārdanaḥ, Krishna, motivator of people

***That God who was seen by me long long ago, the person with the eyes like lotus petals, is your family member, Janārdana Krishna, the motivator of people.***

## Verse 51

अस्यैव वरदानाद्धि स्मृतिर्न प्रजहाति माम्

दीर्घमायुश्च कौन्तेय स्वच्छन्दमरणं तथा (2.51)

**asyaiva varadānāddhi smṛtirna prajahāti mām**
**dīrghamāyuśca kaunteya svacchandamaraṇaṁ tathā**

asyaiva = asya (of this) + eva (even); varadānāddhi = vara (boon) + dānād (dānāt – from being awarded) + dhi (hi – because); smṛtir = smṛtiḥ - memory; na – not; prajahāti – fades; mām – me; dīrgham – long; āyuś = āyuḥ = life; ca – and; kaunteya – son of Kuntī; svacchanda – at one's convenience; maraṇaṁ - death of a body; tathā - so

***Due to the boon given to me by this Deity; my memory does not fade; my lifespan is long; death of my body will occur at my convenience.***

## Verse 52

स एष कृष्णो वार्ष्णेयः पुराणपुरुषो विभुः
आस्ते हरिरचिन्त्यात्मा क्रीडन्निव महाभुजः (2.52)

**sa eṣa kṛṣṇo vārṣṇeyaḥ purāṇapuruṣo vibhuḥ**
**āste hariracintyātmā krīḍanniva mahābhujaḥ**

sa – he; eṣa – this; kṛṣṇo = kṛṣṇaḥ = Krishna; vārṣṇeyaḥ - descendant of Vṛṣṇi; purāṇa – primeval; puruṣo = puruṣaḥ - person; vibhuḥ - Supreme Person; āste – remained, lived; harir = hariḥ = Hari, the person who removes miserable conditions; acintyātmā – inconceivable spirit; krīḍan – the one who plays like a child; niva = iva = as if, like; mahābhujaḥ - greatest of the multi-taskers

***This Krishna, the descendant of Vṛṣṇi, is the Primal Person, the Supreme Person, the one Hari who removes miserable conditions, the inconceivable spirit, the one who plays like a child, the greatest of the multi-taskers.***

## Verse 53

एष धाता विधाता च संहर्ता चैव सात्वतः
श्रीवत्सवक्षा गोविन्दः प्रजापतिपतिः प्रभुः (2.53)

**eṣa dhātā vidhātā ca saṁhartā caiva sātvataḥ**
**śrīvatsavakṣā govindaḥ prajāpatipatiḥ prabhuḥ**

eṣa – this; dhātā – Dhātā; vidhātā – Vidhātā; ca – and; saṁhartā – complete destroyer; caiva – and so; sātvataḥ - a Sātvata relative; śrīvatsa - Śrīvatsa golden curl of hair; vakṣā – chest; govindaḥ - Govinda;

prajāpatipatiḥ - father of the father of the living beings; prabhuḥ - master

***This Krishna is Dhātā and Vidhātā. He is the complete destroyer, a relative of the Sātvata family. He has the Śrīvatsa golden curl of hair on his chest. He is Govinda, the father of the father of the living beings, the master.***

## Verse 54

दृष्ट्वेमं वृष्णिशार्दूलं स्मृतिर्मामियमागता

आदिदेवमजं विष्णुं पुरुषं पीतवाससम् (2.54)

**dṛṣṭvemaṁ vṛṣṇiśārdūlaṁ smṛtirmāmiyamāgatā**
**ādidevamajaṁ viṣṇuṁ puruṣaṁ pītavāsasam**

dṛṣṭvemaṁ = dṛṣṭvā (having seen) + imam (this); vṛṣṇi - Vṛṣṇi; śārdūlaṁ - leader; smṛtir = smṛtiḥ = memory; mām – me; iyam – this; āgatā – surfaced; ādidevam – First and Primary Deity; ajaṁ - the Unborn Person; viṣṇuṁ - God Vishnu; puruṣaṁ - person; pīta – yellow; vāsasam - garment

***Having seen this Krishna, the leader of the Vṛṣṇis, my memory surfaced. He is the First and Primary Deity, the Unborn Person, the God Vishnu, the person who wears yellow garments.***

## Verse 55

सर्वेषामेव भूतानां पिता माता च माधवः

गच्छध्वमेनं शरणं शरण्यं कौरवर्षभाः (2.55)

**sarveṣāmeva bhūtānāṁ pitā mātā ca mādhavaḥ**
**gacchadhvamenaṁ śaraṇaṁ śaraṇyaṁ kauravarṣabhāḥ**

sarveṣām – of all; eva – even; bhūtānāṁ - of the living beings; pitā – father; mātā – mother; ca – and; mādhavaḥ - Krishna, descendant of Madhu; gaccha – go; dhvam – sounding; enaṁ - this; śaraṇaṁ - shelter; śaraṇyaṁ - person to whom one should be reliant on, take shelter; kauravarṣabhāḥ - best of the Kauravas

***Krishna, the descendant of Madhu, is the mother and father of all the living beings. Take recourse of this person who is the one a person should rely on, O best of the Kauravas.***

## Verse 56*

वैशंपायन उवाच

एवमुक्तास्तु ते पार्थां यमौ च पुरुषर्षभौ

द्रौपद्या कृष्णया सार्धं नमश्चक्रुर्जनार्दनम् (3.1)

**vaiśaṁpāyana uvāca**
**evamuktāstu te pārthā yamau ca puruṣarṣabhau**
**draupadyā kṛṣṇayā sārdhaṁ namaścakrurjanārdanam**

vaiśaṁpāyana - Vaiśaṁpāyana; uvāca – said; evam – thus; uktās – said; tu – but; te – you; pārthā – son of Pṛthā; yamau – twin; ca – and; puruṣarṣabhau – two foremost human beings; draupadyā – Draupadī; kṛṣṇayā – to Krishna; sārdhaṁ - with; namaś = namaḥ = offer respectful homage; cakrur = cakruḥ = verification; janārdanam – Krishna, maintainer of the creatures

***Vaiśampāyana said:***

***The sons of Pṛthā and the twin who were foremost among the human beings, along with Draupadī, offered respectful homage to Krishna, who was verified as the maintainer of the creatures.****

**In some editions of the Mahabharata, this verse is the first verse of the next chapter of the text. The author included it since it concludes the incidence of Markendaya's evidence that Krishna is the creator of the world.*

# Index to Narrative Chapters 1-10

# C

# D

# G

# H



# I

# L

# N

# Q, R

# S

# T

# U



# V

# W



# X, Y, Z

# Index to Translated Verses,. Chapters 11&12

## A

# B

# C

**creation**,
process, 3.188.46
repeated, 3.187.17
criminal activity, 3.187.29; 3.188.24
criminal characters, 3.187.55
crocodile, 3.187.68
crow, 3.187.37,67
culture, spiritual self, 3.188.24
curl of hair, 3.187.115; 3.188.53
cycle of time, 3.188.29,34

# D

Danu, 3.187.61,124
death, supervisor, 3.188.17
**Deity**,
Aggregate, 3.187.114
air, 3.188.17
allowance, 3.188.22
altar, 3.187.8
annihilation, 3.188.29
appearance, 3.188.26
boundaries crossed, 3.188.33
Brahmā sleeps, 3.187.76
complexion, 3.187.86
creator, 3.188.12
devilish, 3.188.31
disembodied spirits, 3.188.5
formless, 3.188.34

# E

# F

# G

# H



# I



# J,K

# L

**lifespan**,
short, 3.187.32
virtuous conduct, 3.187.45
**lifestyle**,
righteous, decrease, 3.188.26
socially-destructive, 3.187.44
light of solar flare, 3.188.17
lily, 3.187.67
link to cosmic, 3.187.128
lion, 3.187.106
living beings, small, 3.187.57
lizard, 3.187.68
Lord of the senses, 3.188.33
lotus bed, 3.187.76
lotus-eyed deity, 3.187.83
lotus feet, grasp, 3.187.120
lotus, night blooming, 3.187.67
lotus petal eyes, 3.187.121
lust, free from, 3.188.15-16

# M

Madhu, 3.188.55
magic, 3.188.29
Mahānadī, 3.187.95
Mahendra, 3.187.104
Malaya, 3.187.104
male celestial musicians, 3.187.108
male, ten, father, 3.187.52
Mandara, 3.187.103

# N

# O



# P

# Q,R

ruse and criminal, 3.187.49

# S

sacrifices, deity, 3.187.8
saintly insignia, 3.187.39
Śaka, 3.187.30
Sakra Indra, 3.187.107; 3.188.5
Sātvata, 3.188.53
scatter-brained, 3.187.43
scriptural procedures, 3.187.112
sea monsters, 3.187.97
seeds infertile, 3.187.44
self of it all, 3.188.37
sense of identity, 3.188.15-16
serpent, 3.187.106
serpents, psychic, 3.187.62
servants, women/sex, 3.187.55
Śeṣa, 3.188.10
sexual energy neutralized, 3.188.2
sexual intercourse, 3.187.42
Shiva, 3.188.5
silver ore, 3.187.102
Simhikā, 3.187.108
Sindhu, 3.187.94
snake, uraga, 3.187.64
social association distant, 3.188.15-16
socially-beneficial activity, 3.188.21
solar flares, spread, 3.187.60,63; 3.188.17
Soma, 3.188.5

# T

# U



# V

# About the Author

Michael Beloved (Yogi *Madhvāchārya)* took his current body in 1951 in Guyana. In 1965, while living in Trinidad, he instinctively began doing yoga postures and tried to make sense of the supernatural side of life.

Later in 1970, in the Philippines, he approached a Martial Arts Master named Mr. Arthur Beverford. He explained to the teacher that he was seeking a yoga instructor. Mr. Beverford identified himself as an advanced disciple of *Śrī* Rishi Singh Gherwal, an Ashtanga Yoga master.

Beverford taught the traditional Ashtanga Yoga with stress on postures, attentive breathing and brow chakra centering meditation. In 1972, Michael entered the Denver, Colorado Ashram of *kuṇḍalinī* yoga Master *Śrī* Harbhajan Singh. There he took instruction in bhastrika pranayama and its application to yoga postures. He was supervised mostly by Yogi Bhajan's disciple named Prem Kaur.

In 1979 Michael formally entered the disciplic succession of the Brahmā -Madhava-Gaudiya Sampradaya through *Swāmī* Kirtanananda, who was a prominent sannyasi disciple of the Great Vaishnava Authority *Śrī Swāmī* Bhaktivedanta Prabhupada, the exponent of devotion to Sri Krishna.

However, yoga has a mystic side to it, thus Michael took training and teaching empowerment from several spiritual masters of different aspects of spiritual development. This is consistent with *Śrī* Krishna's advice to Arjuna in the *Bhagavad Gītā*:

*tad viddhi praṇipātena*
*paripraśnena sevayā*
*upadekṣyanti te jñānaṁ*
*jñāninas tattva darśinaḥ*

**This you ought to know. By submitting yourself as a student, by asking questions, by serving as requested, the perceptive, reality-**

> **conversant teachers will teach you the knowledge. (*Bhagavad Gītā* 4.34)**

Most of the instructions Michael received were given in the astral world. On that side of existence, his most prominent teachers were *Śrī Swāmī* Shivananda of Rishikesh, Yogiraj *Swāmī* Vishnudevananda, *Śrī Bābāji Mahasaya* - the master of the masters of *Kriyā* Yoga, *Śrīla* Yogeshwarananda of Gangotri - the master of the masters of *Rāj* Yoga (spiritual clarity), and Siddha *Swāmī* Nityananda the Brahmā Yoga authority.

*Śrī* Rishi Singh Gherwal, who is deceased, inspired this narrative translation of the *Markandeya Samasya*, a small section of the Aranyaka Parva of the *Mahabharata*. Rishi published a translation of this during his life time but that book is now out of print. In the astral world, he requested the writer to translate and present this text in narrative form again.

It is a wonderful tale of a yogi who transcended the mind of the person within whom, that yogi was just an idea. The book solves an existential puzzle.

# Publications

## English Series

Bhagavad Gita English

Anu Gita English

Markandeya Samasya English

Yoga Sutras English

Uddhava Gita English

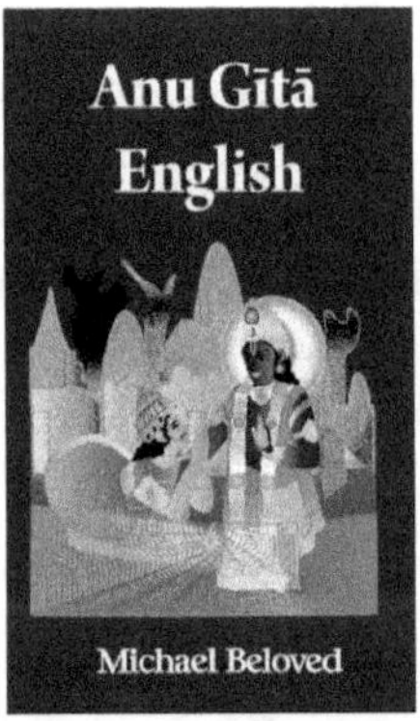

These are in 21st Century English, very precise and exacting. Many Sanskrit words which were considered untranslatable into a Western language are rendered in precise, expressive and modern English, due to the English language becoming the world's universal means of concept conveyance.

Three of these books are instructions from Krishna. **In Bhagavad Gita English** and **Anu Gita English**, the instructions were for Arjuna. In the **Uddhava Gita English,** it was for Uddhava. Bhagavad Gita and Anu Gita are extracted from the Mahabharata. Uddhava Gita was extracted from the 11th Canto of the Srimad Bhagavatam (Bhagavata Purana). One of these books, the **Markandeya Samasya English** is about Krishna, as described by Yogi Markandeya, who survived the cosmic collapse and reached a divine child in whose transcendental body, the collapsed world was existing. Another of these books, the **Yoga Sutras English,** is the detailed syllabus about yoga practice.

My suggestion is that you read **Bhagavad Gita English**, the **Anu Gita English, the Markandeya Samasya English,** the **Yoga Sutras English** and lastly the **Uddhava Gita English**, which is much more complicated and detailed.

For each of these books we have at least one commentary, which is published separately. Thus your particular interest can be researched further in the commentaries.

The smallest of these commentaries and perhaps the simplest is the one for the Anu Gita. We published its commentary as the Anu Gita Explained. The Bhagavad Gita explanations were published in three distinct targeted commentaries. The first is Bhagavad Gita Explained, which sheds lights on how people in the time of Krishna and Arjuna regarded the information and applied it. Bhagavad Gita is an exposition of the application of yoga practice to cultural activities, which is known in the Sanskrit language as karma yoga.

Interestingly, Bhagavad Gita was spoken on a battlefield just before one of the greatest battles in the ancient world. A warrior, Arjuna, lost his wits and had no idea that he could apply his training in yoga to political dealings. Krishna, his charioteer, lectured on the spur of the moment to give Arjuna the skill of using yoga proficiency in cultural dealings including how to deal with corrupt officials on a battlefield.

The second commentary is the Kriya Yoga Bhagavad Gita. This clears the air about Krishna's information on the science of kriya yoga, showing that its techniques are clearly described free of charge to anyone who takes the time to read Bhagavad Gita. Kriya yoga concerns the battlefield which is the psyche of the living being. The internal war and the mental and emotional forces which are hostile to self-realization are dealt with in the kriya yoga practice.

The third commentary is the Brahma Yoga Bhagavad Gita. This shows what Krishna had to say outright and what he hinted about which concerns the brahma yoga practice, a mystic process for those who mastered kriya yoga.

There is one commentary for the **Markandeya Samasya English**. The title of that publication is Krishna Cosmic Body.

There are two commentaries to the Yoga Sutras. One is the Yoga Sutras of Patanjali and the other is the Meditation Expertise. These give detailed explanations of the process of Yoga.

For the Uddhava Gita, we published the Uddhava Gita Explained. This is a large book and requires concentration and study for integration of the information. Of the books which deal with transcendental topics, my opinion is that the discourse between Krishna and Uddhava has the complete information about the realities in existence. This book is the one which removes massive existential ignorance.

# Meditation Series

Meditation Pictorial

Meditation Expertise

Core-Self Discovery

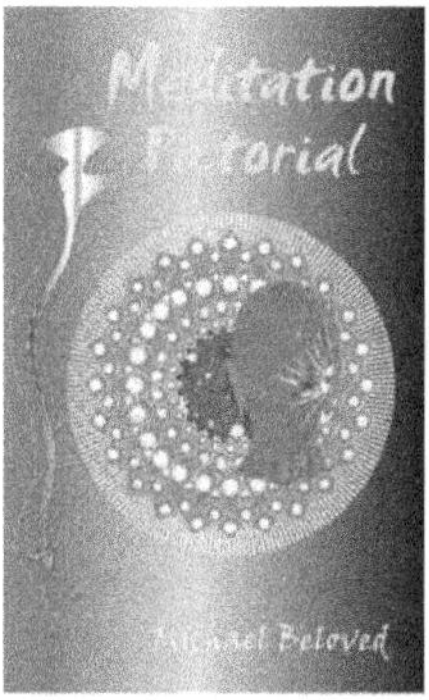

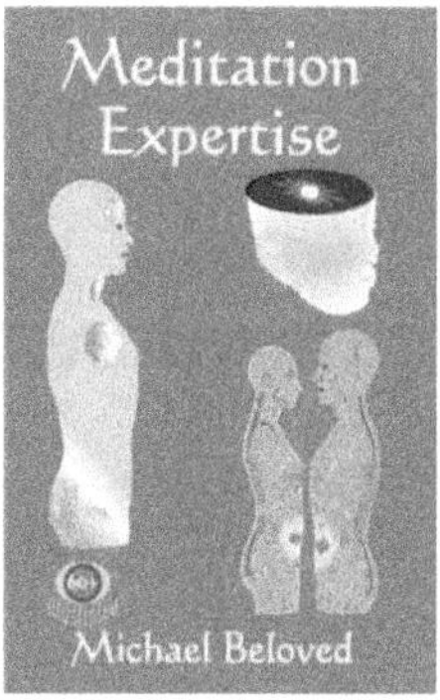

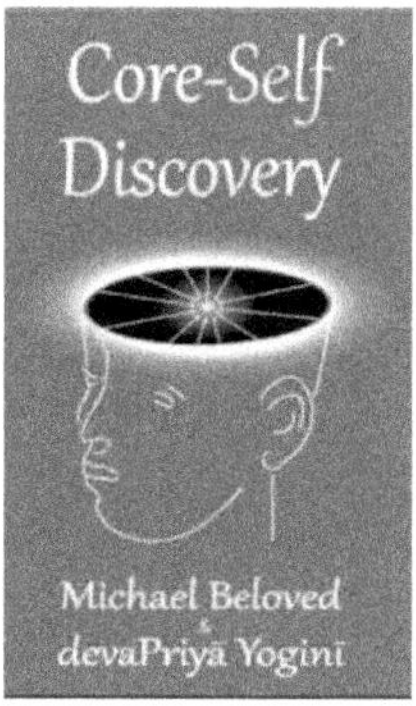


The specialty of these books is the mind diagrams which profusely illustrate what is written. This shows exactly what one has to do mentally to develop and then sustain a meditation practice.

In the **Meditation Pictorial**, one is shown how to develop psychic insight, a feature without which meditation is imagination and visualization, without any mystic experience per se.

In the **Meditation Expertis**e, one is shown how to corral one's practice to bring it in line with the classic syllabus of yoga which Patanjali lays out as the ashtanga yoga eight-staged practice.

In **Core-Self Discovery**, one is taken though the course of pratyahar sensual energy withdrawal which is the 5th stage of yoga in the Patanjali ashtanga eight-process complete system of yoga practice. These events lead to the discovery of a core-self which is surrounded by psychic organs in the head of the subtle body. This product has a DVD component for teachers and self-teaching students.

These books are profusely illustrated with mind diagrams showing the components of psychic consciousness and the inner design of the subtle body.

# Explained Series

Bhagavad Gita Explained

Uddhava Gita Explained

Anu Gita Explained

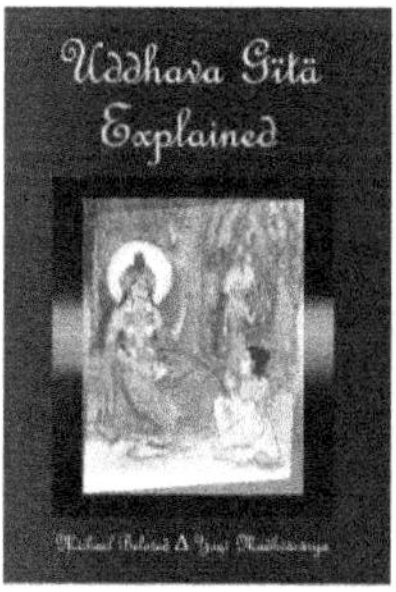

The specialty of these books is that they are free of missionary intentions, cult tactics and philosophical distortion. Instead of using these books to add credence to a philosophy, meditation process, belief or plea for followers, I spread the information out so that a reader can look through this literature and freely take or leave anything as desired.

When Krishna stressed himself as God, I stated that. When Krishna laid no claims for supremacy, I showed that. The reader is left to form an independent opinion about the validity of the information and the credibility of Krishna.

There is a difference in the discourse with Arjuna in the Bhagavad Gita and the one with Uddhava in the Uddhava Gita. In fact these two books may appear to contradict each other. In the Bhagavad Gita, Krishna pressured Arjuna to complete social duties. In the Uddhava Gita, Krishna insisted that Uddhava should abandon the same.

The Anu Gita is not as popular as the Bhagavad Gita but it is the conclusion of that text. Anu means what is to follow, what proceeds. In this discourse, an anxious Arjuna request that Krishna should repeat the Bhagavad Gita and again show His supernatural and divine forms.

However Krishna refuses to do so and chastises Arjuna for being a disappointment in forgetting what was revealed. Krishna then cites a celestial yogi, a near-perfected being, who explained the process of transmigration in vivid detail.

# Commentaries

Yoga Sutras of Patanjali

Meditation Expertise

Krishna Cosmic Body

Anu Gita Explained

Bhagavad Gita Explained

Kriya Yoga Bhagavad Gita

Brahma Yoga Bhagavad Gita

Uddhava Gita Explained

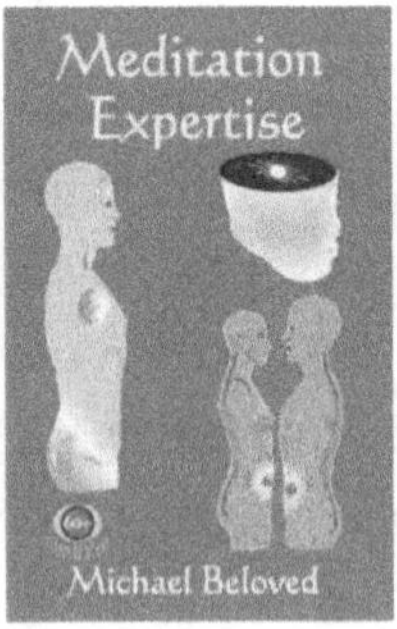

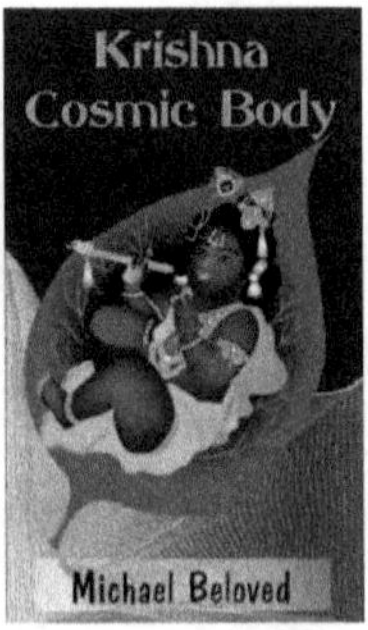

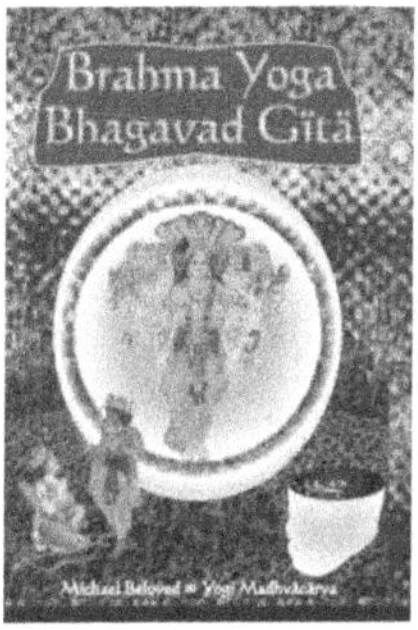

**Yoga Sutras of Patanjali** is the globally acclaimed text book of yoga. This has detailed expositions of yoga techniques. Many kriya techniques are vividly described in the commentary.

**Meditation Expertise** is an analysis and application of the Yoga Sutras. This book is loaded with illustrations and has detailed explanations of secretive advanced meditation techniques which are called kriyas in the Sanskrit language.

**Krishna Cosmic Body** is a narrative commentary on the Markandeya Samasya portion of the Aranyaka Parva of the Mahabharata. This is the detailed description of the dissolution of the world, as experienced by the great yogin Markandeya who transcended the cosmic deity, Brahma, and reached Brahma's source who is the divine infant, Krishna.

**Anu Gita Explained** is a detailed explanation of how we endure many material bodies in the course of transmigrating through various life-forms. This is a discourse between Krishna and Arjuna. Arjuna requested of Krishna a display of the Universal Form and a repeat narration of the Bhagavad Gita but Krishna declined and explained what a siddha perfected being told the Yadu family about the sequence of existences one endures and the systematic flow of those lives at the convenience of material nature.

**Bhagavad Gita Explained** shows what was said in the Gita without religious overtones and sectarian biases.

**Kriya Yoga Bhagavad Gita** shows the instructions for those who are doing kriya yoga.

**Brahma Yoga Bhagavad Gita** shows the instructions for those who are doing brahma yoga.

**Uddhava Gita Explained** shows the instructions to Uddhava which are more advanced than the ones given to Arjuna.

Bhagavad Gita is an instruction for applying the expertise of yoga in the cultural field. This is why the process taught to Arjuna is called karma yoga which means karma + yoga or cultural activities done with a yogic demeanor.

Uddhava Gita is an instruction for apply the expertise of yoga to attaining spiritual status. This is why it is explains jnana yoga and bhakti yoga in detail. Jnana yoga is using mystic skill for knowing the spiritual part of existence.

Bhakti yoga is for developing affectionate relationships with divine beings.

Karma yoga is for negotiating the social concerns in the material world and therefore it is inferior to bhakti yoga which concerns negotiating the social concerns in the spiritual world.

This world has a social environment and the spiritual world has one too.

Right now Uddhava Gita is the most advanced informative spiritual book on the planet. There is nothing anywhere which is superior to it or which goes into so much detail as it. It verified that historically Krishna is the most advanced human being to ever have left literary instructions on this planet. Even Patanjali Yoga Sutras which I translated and gave an application for in my book, **Meditation Expertise**, does not go as far as the Uddhava Gita.

Some of the information of these two books is identical but while the Yoga Sutras are concerned with the personal spiritual emancipation (kaivalyam) of the individual spirits, the Uddhava Gita explains that and also explains the situations in the spiritual universes.

Bhagavad Gita is from the Mahabharata which is the history of the Pandavas. Arjuna, the student of the Gita, is one of the Pandavas brothers. He was in a social hassle and did not know how to apply yoga expertise to solve it. Krishna gave him a crash-course on the battlefield about that.

Uddhava Gita is from the Srimad Bhagavatam (Bhagavata Purana), which is a history of the incarnations of Krishna. Uddhava was a relative of Krishna. He was concerned about the situation of the deaths of many of his relatives but Krishna diverted Uddhava's attention to the practice of yoga for the purpose of successfully migrating to the spiritual environment.

# Specialty

These books are based on the author's experiences in meditation, yoga practice and participation in spiritual groups:

Spiritual Master

sex you!

Sleep **Paralysis**

Astral Projection

Masturbation Psychic Details

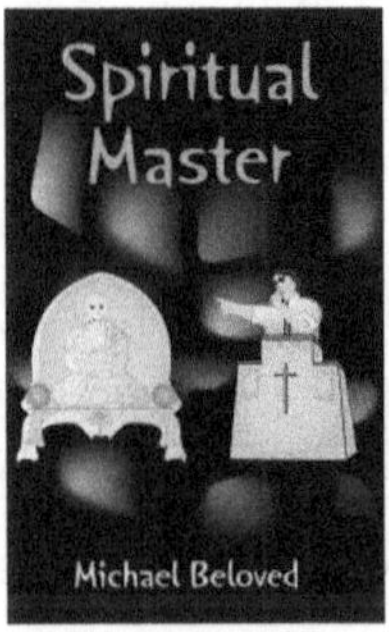

In **Spiritual Master**, Michael draws from experience with gurus or with their senior students. His contact with astral gurus is rated. He walks you through the avenue of gurus showing what you should do and what you should not do, so as to gain proficiency in whatever area of spirituality the guru has proficiency.

**sex you!** is a masterpiece about the adventures of an individual spirit's passage through the parents' psyches. The conversion of a departed soul into a sexual urge is described. The transit from the afterlife to residency in the emotions of the parents is detailed. This is about sex and you; learn about how much of you comprises the romantic energy of your would-be parents!

**Sleep Paralysis** clears misconceptions so that one can see what sleep paralysis is and what frightening astral experience occurs while the paralysis is being experienced. This disempowerment has great value in giving you confidence that you can and do exist even if you are unable to operate the physical body. The implication is that one can exist apart from and will survive the loss of the material body.

**Astral Projection** details experiences Michael had even in childhood, where he assumed incorrectly that everyone was astrally conversant. He discusses the life force psychic mechanism which operates the sleep-wake cycle of the physical form, and which budgets energy into the separated astral form which determines if the individual will have dream recall or no objective awareness during the projections. Astral travel happens on every occasion when the physical body sleeps. What is missing in awareness is the observer status while the astral body is separated.

**Masturbation Psychic Details** is a surprise presentation which relates what happens on the psychic plane during a masturbation event. This does not tackle moral issues or even addictions but shows the involvement of memory and the sure but hidden subconscious mind which operates many features of the psyche irrespective of the desire or approval of the self-conscious personality.

# Online Resources

## Visit The Website And Forum

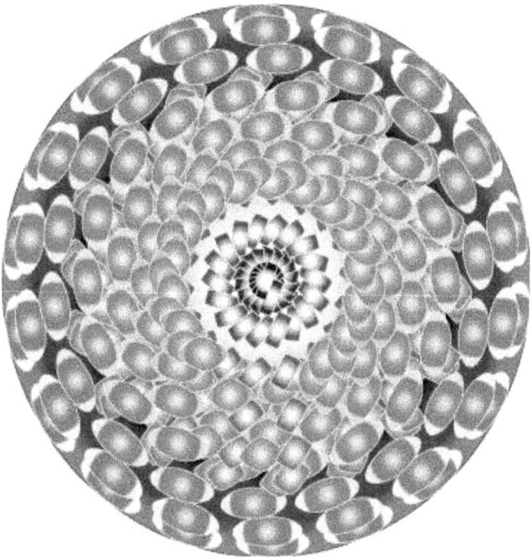

| | |
|---|---|
| ***Email:*** | michaelbelovedbooks@gmail.com<br>axisnexus@gmail.com |
| ***Website*** | michaelbeloved.com |
| ***Forum:*** | inselfyoga.com |

www.ingramcontent.com/pod-product-compliance
Lightning Source LLC
LaVergne TN
LVHW051254080426
835509LV00020B/2964